DISNEOLOGY:

Religious Rhetoric

At

WDW

Stan A. Lindsay

Published by

Say Press

P.O. Box 691063

Orlando, FL 32869-1063

Library of Congress Catalog Card Number

ISBN: 9780984149162

To Esther Lindsay

My Mother--The One Who Gave Me an Appreciation

For the Persuasive Power of Literature

Contents

Preface

I think it will be one of the most enjoyable learning experiences you will have. It is, of course, possible to go to Walt Disney World in Florida and aimlessly absorb the sights and experiences, but for some, the sponge approach is unsatisfactory. Some have already visited Walt Disney World and desire a deeper perspective on the parks. Others have never visited, but desire a logical way of experiencing the parks. Some are, frankly, more interested in rhetoric, philosophy, religion, or science than they are in entertainment. These individuals will find this approach refreshingly different. I recommend that you work through this book, as an introduction to what you will find in the parks, then visit the parks and explore the religious rhetoric and implications that abound.

As a way of making the frequent references to the four parks and the Walt Disney World Resort, as a whole, this book uses the following abbreviations:

WDW is the Walt Disney World Resort.

MK stands for the Magic Kingdom.

AK stands for the Animal Kingdom.

HS is the abbreviation for Disney's Hollywood Studios.

EPCOT stands for Epcot.

As you read through the book, you may wish to use the **Worksheet for Studying this Book** that begins on page 115. The questions are listed in the order in which you will find the material in the text. They help you grasp the important concepts the book teaches.

As you journey through the parks, you may want to use the **Guide for Conducting Park-by-Park Research** that begins on page 127. This guide takes you through the parks, one park at a time, and points out attractions that have something to contribute to your research. Provocative questions are posed, along the way, as you visit attractions.

You will notice that there are **no photos** in this book—yet. That is your job. The thought of gaining all of the necessary permissions from Disney to publish interesting pictures is nightmarish. And, even if it weren't, why would you go to WDW and rely on gaining your memories from someone else's photography? The book recommends certain photos and offers you space in which to attach your photos. You may want to list all of the recommendations, but if you follow the **Guide for Conducting Park-by-Park Research**, you will logically know what photos to take.

Some of the books I have written have been the result of two, five, and even twenty years of research. I can honestly say that this book is the result of over forty years of research and thought. I hope you enjoy reading it as much as I enjoyed writing it.

Stan A. Lindsay, Ph.D.

Panama City Beach, FL

May 1, 2010

Chapter 1

Introduction

What is Disneology? It is an exploration of religious rhetoric at Walt Disney World Resort (WDW). It uses Disney symbols as the starting point for each research learning experience. If archaeology discovers the vast repository of human culture from *past* generations, then Disneology discovers the vast repository of human culture that appeals to many segments of our *current* generation. Where better to explore religious rhetoric than at the most collectively successful cultural repository of our generation? One **definition of rhetoric** is that offered by the ancient Greek philosopher Aristotle: *Rhetoric is the faculty of seeing in each situation the available means of persuasion.* Hence, an exploration of religious rhetoric at WDW will comprise:

- Identifying religious issues raised by symbols at WDW,
- Considering viewpoints of various sides of each issue,

- Looking to see if any positions are available that might allow individuals to reach agreement,
- Checking personally to see if you have been persuaded by one side or another.

The four days we recommend that you spend in the theme parks—plus reading the text and completing worksheets—will provide you with a very substantial learning experience. This book is NOT sponsored by or affiliated with the Walt Disney Corporation. It is NOT related to any internship or international programs that exist at Walt Disney World Resort. Instead, it is designed to offer a directed independent research learning experience. Whether you are a true believer or a skeptic, you will encounter religious rhetoric at WDW, Florida. Lurking in all four theme parks are implicit and explicit religious rhetorical messages. This book will help you find these messages and grapple with your own positions on the religious issues raised by Disney messages.

The objective of this book is not to offer the perspectives, however, of all religions throughout history, or even all religions of the modern world. Clearly, as one will observe through reading this book and visiting WDW, the religion that most strongly influenced Walt Disney was **Christianity**. But, Disney was also influenced by **Science**, and science has historically had some major rhetorical conflicts with religion, in general. Many, if not most, of the religious issues lurking in WDW are disagreements between Christianity and an approach to science that tends to eliminate theological considerations from its messages. Although not all scientists who refrain from discussing theological issues are atheists, some are. **Atheist** rhetorical issues will, therefore, be found in WDW. **Judaism** is encountered in this exploration, but generally in the context of the Hebrew Bible (which is essentially the same as the Christian Old Testament). As Christianity builds on the foundation of Judaism, **Islam** builds on many references to Judaism and Christianity. The Koran refers to Jews and Christians as "People of the Book." Hence, *Disneology*, since it deals largely with religious rhetoric pertaining to issues of the nature and creative acts of God, will afford Muslims opportunities to explore religious issues that are important to them. Because Epcot [EPCOT] contains cultural experiences from around the world adherents of many **other modern religions** may spot religious rhetoric from their culture that this book may not even cover. This book also makes reference to several **religions of the past**, because WDW includes many such religious symbols. This book is an invitation to explore religious issues, to confront religious rhetoric. Any readers who are not as predominantly Judeo-Christian as was Walt Disney (or as is the American culture in which WDW is located), *will be* exposed to Judeo-Christian religious rhetoric. Rhetoric always attempts to persuade. Readers who do not wish to allow themselves to be exposed to such persuasion should *not* continue reading this book.

The Primary Conflict

This book will primarily consider a **central religious conflict** that seems to be present in the mind of Walt Disney, as exemplified in his parks and products. That central religious conflict is the conflict between **Christian Realism** and **Scientific Realism** as it pertains to the origins of the universe, the development of life, and the emergence of humans as the highest life form. **Realism** is based on the proposition: "There is truth." Both Christian Realists and Scientific Realists **agree** with that proposition. Where they **disagree** pertains to *exactly what that truth is*.

The **ISSUES** are many:

- What existed before the universe was formed?

- How did the universe come into being?

- Is there a god?

- What was the chronological sequence in the development of the universe, our solar system, and our planet?

- How long did it take for the world to develop to the stage it has?

- How did life originate?

- What was the chronological sequence in the development of life?

- Did life evolve from species to species? From genus to genus?

- What was the origin of humans?

- Do humans enjoy a special relationship with a divine being?

- Is there life on other planets?

- Is there an afterlife?

Christian Realists and Scientific Realists, more often than not, supply different answers to these questions. Yet, WDW seems to accept the answers of both sides as *truth*. Is this position tenable? Is it possible, as a Realist, to hold both perspectives?

WDW is unafraid to present **religious rhetoric in favor of Christian Realism**. Born in the 19th century, Walt Disney was a huge fan of President **Abraham Lincoln**. Lincoln is the president who receives the greatest attention in the "Hall of Presidents" at the Magic Kingdom [MK]. Disney could have chosen to highlight purely secular comments from Lincoln. Nevertheless, Disney highlights quite religious philosophy, as expressed by Lincoln. His belief in "**divine providence**" is mentioned in his debates. Lincoln **quotes Jesus** from Mark 3:25: "A house divided against itself cannot stand." Lincoln asserts that all men are "**created**" equal. He identifies the Declaration of Independence as the "**truth**." He states his **faith in God**: "I know there is a God and that he hates injustice and slavery. I see a storm coming; I know his hand is in it." Mention of the "creator" in the Declaration of Independence is reiterated in the "American Adventure" in EPCOT. Just outside the "American Adventure," between Thanksgiving and New Years Day, annually, multiple daily presentations of the Candlelight Processional proclaim strong **Christian rhetoric concerning the divine birth of Jesus**. Year-round, Ye Olde Christmas Shoppe, in the MK, **celebrates the Christmas holiday**. Indiana Jones is featured prominently in Disney's Hollywood Studios [HS]. His most famous quest, the search for lost **Ark of the Covenant**, presents viewers with theological concepts of a God who communicates with humans, yet is invisible. Walt also once remarked, "I know drinking and smoking are **sins** because you aren't taking care of the body **God** gave you."

On the other hand, WDW is also unafraid to present **nonreligious rhetoric in favor of Scientific Realism**. The "Universe of Energy" attraction at EPCOT presents the origins of the universe from a wholly god-less perspective. The perspective of **physics** informs riders that originally, there was a "big bang" in which a great amount of energy was converted into huge supplies of mass. Among the pieces of mass that were generated by the big bang was a small piece that became the planet Earth. The perspective of **Geology** (the study of the Earth) then takes over. This originally very hot planet was a fiery, molten, and gaseous mixture. The gasses surrounded the planet until the planet cooled; then, water condensed onto the surface of the earth and became the seas. (Not too many years ago--before they replaced it with "The Seas with Nemo & Friends" ride—WDW had corroborated these views of physics and geology in a preshow to "The Living Seas" exhibit. Again, no mention of a creator was to be found.) The perspective of **Evolutionary Biology** is/was presented in both the Energy and Seas shows, as plant life is followed by water life, then amphibian life, etc. In the 1950s, the *Disneyland* television series on ABC TV aired an episode that presented the history of evolution in a fashion similar to that in which it is shown in the "Rite of Spring" sequence from *Fantasia*. A clip of the scene from *Fantasia* is shown in "The Great Movie Ride" in Disney's HS. Disney apparently believed in evolution. **Paleontology's** perspective (the study of "old things" found in the record of fossils) is presented at the Animal Kingdom [AK], as small children are able to "research" the fossil record at the "Boneyard" playground and along the "Cretaceous Trail." In the attraction "Dinosaur" at the AK, you will time travel backwards to the Cretaceous Era, which the Disney ride estimates, occurred 65 million years ago. Some Christians say this timeline conflicts with a biblical view of the length of time the Earth has existed. While WDW does not carry the paleontology perspective into the realm of **Anthropology**, the study of humans (to offer charts demonstrating the evolutionary ascent of humans from apes), both the "Universe of Energy" ride and "Spaceship Earth" in EPCOT present humans developing culture, beginning with caveman.

Why do many Christians advocate the view that God is the creator of the heavens and the Earth? Many Christians believe that the best biblical scholarship requires this position. This motivation is primarily a **Realistic motivation**. Biblical statements are accepted by many Christians as facts. Facts may be combined into "syllogisms" to establish truth. The term syllogism will be defined later.

Why do many scientists advocate the view that God was *not* involved in the origin and development of the universe, Earth, or life? They believe that the best scientific scholarship requires this position—another Realistic motivation. For both Christian and Scientific Realists, the *truth* must be advocated regardless of the consequences. The belief that "there is truth" is what characterizes a Realist.

Realist Philosophers Throughout History

Plato was a Realist who believed that truth existed in a non-earthly realm of the ideal. He believed that discovering truth was a matter of moving closer and closer to the light. Since all humans existed prior to birth in the ideal realm, they all know the truth but have forgotten it. **Socratic questioning** (explained later in this book) helps humans *unforget* the truth.

Plato's student **Aristotle** saw truth in the *sensory* world rather than in some other-worldly realm. Whatever actually existed in *nature* and was in some process of movement or change was, for Aristotle, true reality.

The seventeenth century philosopher **Rene DesCartes** was a Realist who is credited with founding **Modernism**. His **methodological doubt** suggested that Realists should doubt everything that could be doubted. Whatever is left is truth. This is the basis of the **scientific method**. Scientists make propositions that they are not entirely certain of. These uncertain propositions are called "**hypotheses**." Scientists, then, attempt to systematically "doubt" their hypotheses. They conduct experiments, to see if they can disprove the hypotheses. If they cannot doubt the hypotheses, these hypotheses are considered "truth." **Empiricists**, following DesCartes, suggested that one could doubt everything that is not *empirically verifiable* (capable of being verified by sense-data—seeing, hearing, smelling, tasting, and feeling). Unfortunately, even **empirical evidence** (sense-data) can be doubted, so Empiricism as a Modernist philosophy was largely discredited by the relentless application of methodological doubt. **Mathematics** was the last stronghold of Modernism. When **Kurt Gödel** demonstrated that even mathematics could be doubted—because the whole system proves itself by itself—Modernism effectively crumbled, although **Scientific Realism** still holds modernistic views of reality. In place of Modernism, **Postmodernism** arose. Postmodernism could be called a Realistic philosophy in that it makes a truth claim: typically, "there is *no* truth" or "there is *relative* truth." **Burke** is a Postmodern Realist, but he is not happy with either of these truth-related formulas. In his essay, "The Rhetorical Situation," Burke is much happier with a Postmodern truth-related formula such as "there is *probable* truth." Aristotle teaches that "probable truth" is discovered through *rhetoric*.

Christian Realism is close to Burke's Postmodern view that "there is probable truth." It is also close to Platonic Realism in the sense that it views absolute truth as existing in other-worldly realms. Yet, Christian Realism is not identical with Platonic Realism or any other Realism discussed. Christian Realism believes that there is truth and that such truth has been communicated to humans by God. Christian Realism typically believes that the Old and New Testaments are those true messages communicated from God. Since Christian Realists often agree that the Bible is truth, rhetorically, all truth must be established in Scripture.

Transcendence

Since WDW presents two often conflicting versions of the truth, any attempt to reconcile these versions would be a form of transcendence. **Transcendence** is a sort of *bridge between opposites*. For example, if one person is a Mexican and another person is a Spaniard, they are opposites in *nationality*. One way to "transcend" the fact that they are different is to consider a way in which they are the same. For example, the fact that they both "speak Spanish" transcends their opposite nationality. If one person is a Mexican and another person is an Italian, they are opposites in both *nationality and language*. The fact that they probably both hold the same *religion*—Roman Catholicism—transcends their opposite nationality and language. If one person is a Mexican and another person is an Israeli, they are probably opposites in nationality, language, and religion. Nevertheless, their different religions do share a *common text*. The Old Testament for the Catholic Mexican is the same as the Jewish Israeli's Bible. If one person is a

Scientific Realist from the United States and another person is a Christian Realist from Mexico, they may be opposites in nationality, language, and religion, but they share the same basic type of *philosophy*—Realism.

Whenever a group of people, such as scientists, identify with one another, there is "**identification**." This means there is a sense of **unity** felt by all members of the group. This unity, however, is usually accomplished by **dissociating** with other groups. In other words, scientists may see themselves as a group dissociated from religionists or politicians, etc. This means there is a sense of **division** felt by all members of the group—division from other groups. When one group attempts to persuade another group that membership in their group is to be preferred, the group uses **rhetoric** to effect the persuasion.

In *A Rhetoric of Motives*, page 25, Burke teaches that dissociation (or division) and unification (or identification) may frequently be transcended by rhetoric: "But put identification and division ambiguously together, so that you cannot know for certain just where one ends and the other begins, and you have the characteristic invitation to rhetoric."

Since transcendence unifies dissociations, it is characteristically rhetorical. This book will explore ways to transcend the divisions between Scientific Realism and Christian Realism in the symbols of WDW. It is an objective of this book not only to locate those divisions (the areas in which the two Realistic approaches disagree) between Scientific Realism and Christian Realism, but also to offer ways of transcending those divisions. Rhetoric is the methodology used to transcend division and produce unification.

Theology

Chapter 2

Who is God (as compared to humans)?

The New World Encyclopedia (http://www.newworldencyclopedia.org/entry/God) states:

> "Throughout history, the vast majority of people in the world have believed in a God. Yet, although notions of an absolute divine power are found in virtually all of the world's religions, the precise definition of what God is . . . varies greatly among the religions, within specific sects, and even from person to person. Typically, monotheistic theology describes God as omniscient, omnipotent, and omnipresent (and in most theologies, immutable), as well as both the creator and sustainer of the universe."

One way of viewing what God might be like is to consider the greatest humans the world has ever known and subtract out all the frailties and limitations. The reverse of this process is called **anthropomorphism**, from the Greek words *anthropos* (meaning man/human) and *morphē* (meaning form/shape). When humans attribute their own characteristics to God, they anthropomorphize. They *reduce* God, in a sense. Similar reduction occurs when physicians refer to their patients only in terms of their specific ailments—the hematoma in Room 212, the C-section in Room 533. Kenneth Burke sees such **reduction** in Behaviorism, as Behaviorists reduce humans to sheer animals, while Burke argues that humans are a unique variety of animal; they should not be so reduced. Humans are **symbol-using** (symbol-making, symbol-misusing) animals. Other animals communicate using **signals**, as opposed to **symbols**. Future chapters will contain more about this symbol use. For now, the comment is offered to demonstrate a religious issue: In defining God, there is, first, the *reductionist approach* of anthropomorphism. Yet, another approach may also be considered--in the opposite direction from reductionism (in the opposite direction from anthropomorphism). Instead of *reducing* God *to* human traits, one might *elevate* God *from* human traits. As an example of this approach, the Dedication to the book *Implicit Rhetoric: Kenneth Burke's Extension of Aristotle's Concept of Entelechy* reads: "To God, the Ultimate Symbol-User."

Some of the *limitations of humans* are implied in the famous theological descriptive terms— omniscient, omnipotent, eternal, omnipresent, and immutable.

- **Immutable** means that, while humans change constantly, God is unchangeable; he is the same—yesterday, today, and forever.

- **Omnipresent** means that, while humans can only be in one place at a time, God is not confined to any single location at any specific time; he is present everywhere in the universe at all times.

- **Eternal** means that, while humans are time-bound (they are born, they live a while, and they die), God has no beginning and no end.

- **Omnipotent** means that, while humans have been able to harness the energy of the Earth to send spacecraft to the Moon, Mars, and beyond, this power is infinitesimal compared to a God who created the entire universe (of which man's space exploration has only scratched the surface).

- **Omniscient** means that, while humans know many things, God knows all things.

Humans are neither immutable nor omnipresent. No humans are eternal. A few, such as Enoch and Elijah from the Bible, are said to have never died, but they certainly were said to have been born. Hence, they are not eternal in *both* temporal directions. Powerful humans, throughout history, have sometimes been thought of as gods—Hercules, Alexander the Great, the Pharaohs of Egypt, Roman Emperors, etc. Yet, all of these powerful humans eventually fell. The humans, throughout history, whom society has termed "**geniuses**," have been those who seemed to know more things that most other humans. While not being thought of as gods, *Albert Einstein, Aristotle, Sigmund Freud, Thomas Edison, Leonardo DaVinci, William Shakespeare,* and *Wolfgang Mozart* have been monumental figures in history. To this list of recognized geniuses, let us add the names of a lesser-known genius—*Kenneth Burke*—and a very well-known genius—*Walt Disney*.

Assignment #1: Visit the attraction "The American Adventure" at EPCOT (and/or the attraction "Carousel of Progress" in the MK). Make a list of the geniuses you see or hear referenced in the presentation. Why do you think of these individuals as geniuses? What did they "know" that the average human does not?

None of these geniuses are gods. They all have/had significant **frailties and limitations**. Even - the Greek part-human-part-god, *Hercules*, is depicted as a glutton and drinker, "capable of random outbursts of brutal rage" (http://www.essortment.com/all/herculesgreekh_rmgk.htm). *Alexander the Great* was a megalomaniac. The Bible depicts terrible atrocities committed by the *Pharaohs* and various *Roman Emperors*. *Sigmund Freud* was a heavy cigar smoker who developed oral cancer. *Thomas Edison* was an early participant in film piracy. In 1902, his agents obtained a copy of a copy of "A Trip to the Moon" by Georges Méliès. He made multiple copies and showed it in America before Méliès could. This eventually bankrupted Méliès. *Albert Einstein* divorced his first wife and married his cousin. *Kenneth Burke* divorced his first wife and married her sister. Burke drank too much and spoke in vulgarities. By contrast, *Walt Disney* often opposed drinking. His theme parks did not market alcoholic beverages during his lifetime. His movie *Pinocchio* featured a conscience for Pinocchio, named Jiminy Cricket (a *euphemism for "Jesus Christ"*) steering the puppet away from alcohol, smoking, and truancy. Christian Filmmakers Academy faculty member Geoffrey Botkin observes: "Budding filmmakers will study Walt's mastery of cutting-edge technology and classic storytelling and the '19th century values'--monogamy, faithfulness, patriotism and virtue--that infused his stories" (http://www.reuters.com/article/industryNews/idUSN1835715920071024). Nevertheless, the same academy criticized the Walt Disney Corporation for its gay-friendly policies and for its production of such movies as "Priest," "Dogma," and "Pulp Fiction," after Walt's death.

While these geniuses had faults, they also were significant **creators**—a primary epithet applied to God. Consider the **artistic creations** of DaVinci, Mozart, Shakespeare, and Disney. Think of the discoveries of Einstein, Freud, Aristotle, and Burke. Ponder the inventions of Edison. Their individual contributions affect all who live in the modern world. Yet, this book has chosen to consider the genius Walt Disney as a point of reference for an analysis of religious rhetoric. When we think of God as *omniscient,* our best examples of human genius are suitable points of reference. Among these geniuses, Disney stands out as the most well-known to contemporary audiences of all ages and cultures. The Christian Filmmakers Academy, referenced earlier as criticizing the Walt Disney Corporation, observes that Disney "exercises an alarmingly vast global influence." WDW in Florida is the number #1 tourist destination in the world. Disney artistic creations are probably better known by all contemporary ages and cultures than those of DaVinci, Mozart, or Shakespeare. Disney even pays tribute to the genius of others throughout his theme parks and motion pictures. I have a good grasp of the genius of Disney. I reside in Florida. Even when I lived in the Midwest, I made annual trips to Florida. My wife and I honeymooned in Florida in 1970, just as WDW was being built. Whether our home was in Iowa, Illinois, or Indiana, we travelled each year to Florida and WDW. All of my four children and my daughter-in-law have worked for WDW. I have also travelled to *Disneyland* in Anaheim and to *Disneyland Paris*. I know the parks and the creative productions of Disney. I think it will be fun to view religious rhetoric through Disney symbols. Those who travel to Orlando with their families may find, in this book, opportunities to discuss theology, philosophy, and rhetoric as they visit Disney locations.

Readers should wear no blinders. They should be fully aware of the religious and philosophical criticisms of the Walt Disney Corporation. This approach is not an attempt to discover or endorse the theology or philosophy of Walt Disney. Yet, even when one disagrees strongly with the theology implicit or explicit in WDW, one at least encounters the issue with which one disagrees. One has an opportunity to explore the pertinent theology, philosophy, and rhetoric as each issue arises.

What, then, is Disneology? It is an exploration of theology, philosophy, and rhetoric. It uses Disney symbols as the starting point for each issue. Disneology discovers the vast repository of human culture that appeals to many segments of our current generation. Where better to explore theology and philosophy than at the most collectively successful cultural repository of our generation?

Photos of "The American Adventure" at EPCOT and "Carousel of Progress" in the MK

More Photos

Chapter 3

Imagine that You Were God!

Assignment #2: Visit the attraction "Walt Disney: One Man's Dream" at HS. Make a list of the inventions, innovations, and "creations" of Walt Disney. What, do you think, is the driving motivation for the man who created the Disney Empire? What is the glue that holds together everything he built in his lifetime? Why did he do all these things?

What would you DO, if you were God?

- If you were unrestricted in terms of resources (you owned everything),
- If you were unrestricted in terms of power (you were omnipotent),
- If you were unrestricted by time (you were eternal),
- If you were unrestricted by knowledge (you knew everything; you were omniscient),

What would you do?

This book is using Walt Disney as a representative anecdote. Walt had restrictions in resources; he declared bankruptcy on October 4, 1923, and was nearly bankrupt a few other times. He had restrictions in power, time, and knowledge; yet, he DID something. What did he do and why did he do it? Kenneth Burke offers a way of analyzing Walt Disney's motives: Burke's **Pentad**. I devote a chapter of *Implicit Rhetoric: Kenneth Burke's Extension of Aristotle's Concept of Entelechy* to explaining how the Pentad works, but (very simply) it proposes that human behavior be viewed as Drama. Every drama requires **acts** that must be performed within **scenes**. The acts are performed by **agents** who use certain tools or methods (**agencies**) to perform the acts. These four terms are easily remembered by thinking of the game "Clue." The *act* in Clue is given; it was the "killing of Mr. Body." Players must determine the *agent*. Was it Colonel Mustard, Miss Peacock, Professor Plum? They must determine what *agency* was used by the agent—a knife, lead pipe, rope, revolver, wrench, etc. The players must also determine the *scene* in which the killing takes place. Was Mr. Body killed in the kitchen, conservatory, ballroom, study, or library? What is not included in the game of Clue is the **purpose**. Why did Colonel Mustard kill Mr. Body in the kitchen with the knife? Was Mrs. Mustard cheating on her husband with Mr. Body? Was Mr. Body stealing from or blackmailing Colonel Mustard? Did Mr. Body attack Colonel Mustard, thus forcing Mustard to kill Body in self-defense? Consistency demands an answer. Drama demands that, in the final analysis, we understand how all parts of the drama fit together.

Consider the accomplishments of Walt's life as one primary *act*. Walt's consummate act was the production of the most successful family entertainment entity in the world. You listed the elements of this consummate act—his inventions, innovations, and "creations"—in your completion of Assignment #2. What do all of these elements have in common?

In what *scene* did Walt's act take place? The answer to this question is two-fold. There was Scene 1—the circumstances that prompted Walt to produce his empire. This scene included personal, family, and national *hardships* described in the film you viewed at the conclusion of your visit to "Walt Disney: One Man's Dream." Scene 2 is the scene Walt personally produced—Disneyland, Walt Disney World, the various motion pictures, etc. Producing Scene 2 involved, technically, several of Walt's individual *acts*.

What sort of *agent* was Walt? While his theme parks prohibited drinking, Walt personally drank too much. While his movies are usually rated G, his own language would have often earned him an R rating. While his Pinocchio character eschewed drinking and smoking, whiskey and chain-smoking are the agencies that killed Walt. He once remarked, "I know drinking and smoking are **sins** because you aren't taking care of the body **God** gave you." Nevertheless, he never changed his behavior. Walt, however, should not be reduced (as an agent) to his vices or his virtues. Consider what his unique character was like (as in a drama). Our goal is not to view Walt as a god, but only to consider how elaborate and consistent God's creation would be by comparing it with the elaborate-yet-consistent inventions and innovations of the genius Walt Disney. We should consider what type of human would do the things that Walt did. There is an **agent-act ratio** to consider. What kinds of agents perform what kinds of acts?

Technology was the *agency* used most by Walt. Other primary agencies were classical music and classic literature. Motion pictures had been around for awhile, but no one had used high quality artistry and combined it with motion pictures and classic literature to produce something like *Snow White and the Seven Dwarfs*. While the technology always seemed to be cutting edge, Walt did not pursue technology for technology's sake.

So, why did Walt do what he did? What was his *purpose*? According to Walt Disney, his dream of Disneyland was prompted by his social nature (a nature which, incidentally, biblical texts also impute to God). Walt cites as his motive for creating Disneyland his experience with his own daughters. He found himself taking the children to a park, and then sitting idly on the sidelines while his children played. He thought it would be wonderful if there were a Scene in which adults and children (Agents) could do things together (Act). He therefore used technology, money, and Imagineering (Agencies) to create Disneyland—his new Scene. Why? He (Agent) created (Act) Disneyland (Scene) with money, technology, and Imagineering (Agencies) in order that families could socialize (Purpose). He wanted adults and children to do happy things together.

The point of this chapter, however, is to imagine what would motivate God, from a Christian Realist perspective. The first chapter of Genesis indicates the prime Agent **who**, according to Genesis, was acting—God/*Elohim*. The same chapter indicates **what** the Judeo-Christian God *did* (Act). He created the heavens and the Earth and all that dwell on Earth. Chapter 1 indicates **how** God did what he did. He used spoken Word (Agency). Chapter 1 describes the **where**, the Scene into which the God of Genesis brought order—formlessness and void (the *Tohu* and *Bohu* of the Hebrew text). The second chapter of Genesis offers a glimpse into **why** God did this act. Apparently, it was his social nature (Purpose). We see a picture of God walking with Adam and Eve in the cool of the evening. We see God asking Adam to be his collaborator. Adam is invited to name the animals God created. We see God understanding that Adam, himself, was lonely. He needed a companion, Eve. We see God as a parent figure, setting limitations. We see him disappointed when his newly-formed creatures-in-His-own-image distrust him and violate the limitations he set. Much later in the Bible, John expresses this biblical God's purpose in one of the most famous verses in the New Testament—John 3:16. "For God so *loved* the world, that he gave his only begotten son . . . ."

So, that's the biblical account. There are many other accounts of gods, many of whom various symbols in WDW represent. What kind of Agent does what kind of Act? Imagine that you were God. What would you DO?

Photos of "Walt Disney: One Man's Dream" at HS

Physics

Chapter 4

Dinosaurs, Young Earth, Old Earth?

Assignment #3: Visit the attraction "Universe of Energy" at EPCOT. Starting with the "Big Bang," in a very short span of time, you will view a sequence of events that many scientists believe occurred over a period of 13 to 14 billion years. What you are viewing is Disney's visual interpretation of the origins of the universe, according to accepted views in physics. Did the universe actually take that long to develop? If you have not yet seen enough dinosaurs, visit the attraction "Dinosaur" at the AK. There, you will time travel backwards to the Cretaceous Era, which the Disney ride estimates occurred 65 million years ago. Has the Earth been around that long?

Creationism is a term often embraced by Judeo-Christian conservatives and often reviled by religious and secular liberals. The term refers to *a philosophy of the origins of the universe in which an agent (God) is actively involved in the formation of everything in the universe.* As suggested in a previous chapter, the presence of an Agent implies an Act, a Scene, an Agency, and a Purpose. The scientific theory presented in the "Universe of Energy" seems to lack an

Agent. Hence, it could be inferred that the origin of the universe was *not* an Act. It had no Scene, required no Agency, and *had no purpose*. Small wonder that Christian Realists are hesitant to overwhelmingly embrace this view of the origins of our universe! Indeed, this view of origins is clearly capable of supplying a strong motive for some to reject science altogether— to pursue a purely antagonistic stance. Many Christian Realists have been tempted, therefore, to "throw the baby out with the bath water." This ISSUE sparks debate not only *between* Christian Realists and Scientific Realists, but also *among* Christian Realists.

Some atheists, agnostics, and Bible-believers have asserted that the Bible teaches that the universe (heavens and Earth) came into being in six twenty-four hour periods, not 13 billion years. They say that, according to the Bible, the entire process began approximately 6000 years ago, beginning with the six days of creation. Those who believe that are called **Young Earth** advocates. To support the Young Earth believers' view—countering "scientific" evidence of fossil remains, carbon dating, etc.—Young Earth advocates pose the question: "How old did Adam appear when God created him?" Did he look as if he were 25? Then, if God can create a man who, though newly crafted, appeared to look 25 years old, he could create a universe that appears to look 13 billion years old (even though it is really only 6000 years old). True enough, if you accept the premise that God created Adam to appear to be 25. The **syllogism** works, if the **premises** are accepted:

- **Major Premise**: God can create things to appear much older than they are.
- **Minor Premise**: The universe appears to be much older than 6000 years.
- **Conclusion**: God can create the universe to appear much older than 6000 years.

The syllogism is the basis of **deductive reasoning**. It comprises a general fact (Major Premise), a specific fact (Minor Premise), and a "deduction." The deduction is called a "conclusion," and is based upon the logical result of accepting the two facts in the two premises. The reasoning present in the syllogism presented above is, of course, tied to the definition of God as omnipotent. Some do *not* accept the Major Premise of the syllogism, but those who believe God to be *omnipotent* have no problem with the premise. Yet, some Christian Realists, while they might accept the premise, wonder about the **extended syllogism**, concerning the Biblical teaching. They question whether the premise is actually true that "the Bible teaches that the universe (heavens and Earth) came into being in six twenty-four-hour periods, not 13 billion years." Are all Christian Realists inextricably bound to a view that is in such disharmony with current scientific views? Can this "division" be "transcended?" Consider the rhetoric:

In the Introduction to my book *Persuasion, Proposals, and Public Speaking* (2nd edition), the analytical method of **Stephen Toulmin** is demonstrated. Toulmin extends the syllogism by providing for situations in which some of the premises or conclusions might not be true. The book uses the O. J. Simpson trials as examples of Toulminian analysis. In this situation, let's try to apply **Toulminian analysis** to the view that the heavens and Earth are only thousands of years old.

Certainly, it is possible to interpret the Genesis account of creation as stating that the entire universe and its inhabitants (up to and including humans) were completely created in six twenty-four-hour periods, just a few thousand years ago. This translation is possible because the word "day" (*yom*, in the Hebrew) most frequently refers to "one twenty-four-hour period." We could submit the Toulminian **Claim** that the Bible possibly teaches that the universe is a few thousand years old. Nevertheless, Toulminian analysis next permits us to attempt a **Rebuttal**. A rebuttal *typically begins with the word "unless."* So, here is one rebuttal: "*unless* the term day/*yom* can mean something other than a twenty-four-hour period." As it turns out, that is the case. In addition to the twenty-four hour denotation, the word *yom* also, at times, simply means "light," as opposed to "darkness" (Genesis 1:5).

Yom also refers to time periods other than the twenty-four-hour variety. According to the first chapter of Genesis, God created man—both male and female—and gave them instructions to multiply and fill the Earth, all in one *yom* (Day Six). In the second chapter of Genesis, there is an expanded discussion of several steps in this process. First, God creates Adam, a male, and instructs him to keep the Garden of Eden, to name the animals, to refrain from eating of the Tree of the Knowledge of Good and Evil, etc. Then, God notices Adam's loneliness, brings a deep sleep upon him, removes a rib from his side, fashions it into a female (Eve), and brings her to Adam. Later (when Adam and Eve are not together), a serpent successfully induces Eve to eat from the Tree, and Eve subsequently successfully tempts Adam to do so. They invent clothing and hide from God. God discovers them and interrogates them. They are cast from the Garden of Eden and *finally* told to be fruitful and multiply in the Earth. These are quite a few events to have all been completed in one twenty-four-hour period. Nevertheless, Genesis 5:1-2 confirms that Adam and Eve were created in a *yom*.

Consider another example of *yom* lasting longer than twenty-four hours. In Genesis 2:17, God tells Adam that "in the day you eat" from the Tree of Knowledge of Good and Evil, you shall surely die. Since (according to Genesis 5:8) Adam lived 930 years, the *yom* in which he ate and died appears to be quite long. In fact, this nearly-one-thousand-year-long *yom* appears to be close to the famous formula found in Psalm 90:4: "For a thousand years are in [God's] eyes as a *yom*." Changing the Hebrew word *yom*/day to the Greek term *hemera*/day, Second Peter 3:8 declares: "One *day* with the Lord is as a thousand years, and a thousand years is as one *day*."

There may be an *answer* to the *rebuttal* that Adam died in the *yom* in which he ate from the tree of Knowledge of Good and Evil. That answer would pertain to the definition of another curious theological word: "die." Science tells us that our bodies are constantly experiencing death. Cells are constantly dying and being regenerated. If one argues that, prior to eating of the Tree of Knowledge of Good and Evil, Adam and Eve's bodies were *immortal* (and not even their cells were dying), the eating of the forbidden fruit, it may be argued, could have triggered the mortality factor. In other words, not only in the same twenty-four-hour period did Adam and Eve experience the death process, it may have begun as early as the very *moment* they ate. This argument would be phrased by Toulmin as a **Backing**. A backing rebuts the rebuttal, in a sense. It typically begins with the word "*but*." So, a Toulminian sequence might look like this:

- **Warrant**: The definition of "day" is a twenty-four hour period.
- **Data**: Genesis claims that the world was created in six days.
- **Claim**: God created the universe in six twenty-four-hour periods.
- **Rebuttal**: *Unless* the "day" in which Adam died lasted 930 years.

- **Backing**: *But*, Adam may have technically "died" (or begun the dying process) at the very moment he ate.
- **Qualifier**: *possibly*

As you can see, the **Warrant** of Toulmin is quite similar to the *Major Premise* of the syllogism. It is a general statement of **fact** (something almost universally accepted). The **Data** of Toulmin represent a specific statement of fact. Therefore, the term *data* is nearly equivalent to the *Minor Premise* of the syllogism. For Toulmin, the **Claim** is similar to the *Conclusion* of the syllogism, except that the term "conclusion" is too conclusive. Toulmin reduces it to a "claim" because, using a less sure connotation (claim, instead of conclusion), it then becomes susceptible to attack. A **Rebuttal** is an attack on either the *warrant* or the *data* or the *claim* or the *backing*. The *rebuttal* listed above is an attack on the *warrant*. It is saying: "The definition of 'day' is a twenty-four hour period *unless* the 'day' in which Adam died lasted 930 years." The backing, then, attacks the rebuttal: *But*, Adam may have technically "died" (or begun the dying process) at the very moment he ate (hence, he *did* die in that twenty-four-hour period). The Toulminian **Qualifier** is an adverb (such as *possibly*, *probably*, or *definitely*) that indicates the strength of the claim. The qualifier is inserted between the subject and the verb of the claim, thus: God *possibly* created the universe in six twenty-four-hour periods.

A third example of *yom* lasting longer than twenty-four hours is found in Genesis 2:4. This verse seems to suggest that *all* of creation—heavens, Earth, plants, animals, and humans—occurred in a single *yom*. Even those who suggest that God created all things in 144 hours are hesitant to assert that it all happened within twenty-four hours.

While sound biblical scholarship certainly permits the interpretation that the heavens and Earth and all varieties of inhabitants were formed in 144 hours, this is not the *only* possible interpretation. Those who wish to discredit either the Bible or science on that basis may be mistaken. If the division can be transcended, Walt Disney may consistently hold to both the Christian Realist and the Scientific Realist (Physics) version of the truth. It is highly doubtful that Disney thought through all of this, but this book is only an exploration of the rhetorical issues that arise.

Furthermore, a *second rebuttal* may be advanced against the claim that the Bible teaches that the universe is a few thousand years old. This rebuttal may be phrased: "*unless* the first word of the Bible has been mistranslated." The first word of the Bible in the original language of Hebrew is *bereshit*. It is almost always translated: "In the beginning." There is, however, a problem with that translation. The problem lies in the fact that the term *bereshit* is a Hebrew **"construct" form**. This means that the term "beginning" should be connected with another noun by the word "of." The second word of Genesis is *not*, however, a noun; it is the word *bara'*, a verb, translated "He created." Among the possible solutions to this translation problem, Hebrew scholars have suggested that the *textual helps* that lead us to see this as a verb may be mistaken. (These textual helps were not in the original written Hebrew text.) It is quite permissible, if the textual helps are removed, to read *bara'* as a noun (or Gerund): "the creating." This is how the translation of Genesis 1:1-2 might, thus, read: "In the Beginning of God's creating the heavens and the Earth, the Earth was formless and void.

If the translation just offered is correct, we do not know for certain exactly where the Genesis creation account purports to begin. What is the exact point in the beginning of creating that the first day described in Genesis actually begins? It is somewhere in the beginning, but the Earth is apparently already in existence, albeit in a formless and chaotic state. Of course, this is not the *only* possible translation/interpretation of Genesis 1:1-2, but *neither* is the translation: "In the beginning God created the heavens and the Earth."

Those Christian Realists who choose to interpret the Genesis account of creation as occurring within a very short time span have some reasonable (syllogistic) basis for taking that position. Yet, those who believe the heavens and Earth took a much longer time to develop need not throw the baby out with the bath water. Young Earth and Old Earth both have possibilities in Judeo-Christian theology. Toulmin just shows how the various arguments are made. Those who contend that God is truly *eternal* may even find this issue irrelevant. The rhetorical issue is not only something that might spark debate *between* Christian Realists and Scientific Realists (**external rhetoric**); it is also a rhetorical issue *among* Christian Realists (**internal rhetoric**). Religious rhetoric at WDW includes both internal and external religious rhetoric.   WDW could not remain consistent, however, if it accepted a Young Earth position. The Scientific Realism position presented in the parks is an Old Earth position. Therefore, while WDW presents God as creator, you will not find at WDW any rhetoric about that creation occurring 6000 years ago or during six twenty-four-hour periods.

Beyond the consideration of how rhetorical divisions might be transcended, an important contribution of this chapter is its aid in understanding how the **rhetorical analysis of Stephen Toulmin** may be used in the process.

Photos of the "Big Bang" sequence at the "Universe of Energy" at EPCOT

(Note: Certain attractions, such as the "Universe of Energy" prohibit the use of flash photography and videography. If you have a night setting on your camera, you might be allowed to use it in such situations. The light from the projected movies should be sufficient to allow you to capture the picture.)

Chapter 5

The "Big Bang," Einstein, and Aristotle?

Assignment #4: If you don't remember everything from the last assignment, visit the attraction "Universe of Energy" at EPCOT again. This time, pay very close attention to what Bill Nye, the science guy, calls the "big bang" and Ellen calls the "ding dang." If a sculptor plans to sculpt a statue, s/he must decide whether to sculpt it out of soap, ice, rock, gold, bronze, wood, etc. What "material" was used to form the universe, according to the film? Hint: it may be related to the name of the attraction.

Two thousand three hundred years before Burke explained his Pentad, with its Agent and Purpose, another genius, **Aristotle**, contended that there was purpose in the **natural world**.

Aristotle's term for **Purpose** was one of Aristotle's **four major causes of action**. *Telos* is known as the **Final Cause**—the purpose for which things in nature occur. Aristotle also saw an **Agent** in the natural world--the person, force, or cause that began the act. *Archē* is known as the **Efficient Cause**. Aristotle taught that the agent/*archē* used a third type of cause to accomplish the purpose. *Hulē* is known as the **Material Cause**. I explain how these causes of Aristotle relate to Kenneth Burke's views in my book, *Implicit Rhetoric: Kenneth Burke's Extension of Aristotle's Concept of Entelechy*. Here, I especially want to emphasize the Material Cause— *hulē*. THE ISSUE: If God created the heavens and the Earth, what material did he create them out of? Was there some sort of **preexisting material** (*hulē*) that God used?

Theologians since the second century a.d. have debated whether the universe was created *ex nihilo* (out of nothing), *ex materia* (out of some preexisting material), or *ex deo* (out of God's nature itself). If you hold the position (mentioned as a possibility in a previous chapter) that the exact point in the beginning of creating that the first day described in Genesis is somewhere in the beginning, but the Earth is apparently already in existence, albeit in a formless and chaotic state, it is possible (but not necessary) to hold an *ex materia* Christian Realist position. Actually, you are not required, by accepting this translation, to hold any specific position on the origin of the material used to form the universe. You could also hold an *ex nihilo* or an *ex deo* Christian Realist position. Frankly, if you accept this translation, you could even hold an **agnostic** position on this issue, and still be a Christian Realist. You could say that the Bible does not tell us, so we "do not know" (the meaning of the term *agnostic*).

On the other hand, for Christian Realists, there is John's creation theology in the first chapter of his gospel. Even if Genesis 1:1 does not absolutely commit Christian Realists to a position that the material world is not eternal, the first chapter of John seems to do the trick, at least for Christian Realists: "In the beginning was the Word, and the Word was with God, and the Word was God. The same was in the beginning with God. By [the Word] all things came into being. And without [the Word] nothing was made that was made."

This is where Ellen's "Ding Dang," Bill Nye's "Big Bang," **Einstein's E=MC²**, Aristotle's *hulē*, Disney's "Universe of Energy," and Kenneth Burke's **Logology** could feasibly converge (or be transcended). And, theological discussions of *ex nihilo*, *deo*, and *materia* are not far removed from this issue. According to Einstein, **Mass** (or Aristotle's *hulē*) can be changed into **Energy**, and vice versa. Einstein explains his **theory of relativity**, as follows:

> It followed from the special theory of relativity that mass and energy are both but different manifestations of the same thing -- a somewhat unfamiliar conception for the average mind. Furthermore, the equation E is equal to m c-squared, in which energy is put equal to mass, multiplied by the square of the velocity of light, showed that very small amounts of mass may be converted into a very large amount of energy and vice versa. The mass and energy were in fact equivalent, according to the formula mentioned above. This was demonstrated by Cockcroft and Walton in 1932, experimentally.

You may listen to Einstein make this statement "in his own voice" at http://www.aip.org/history/einstein/voice1.htm.

The **Big Bang** theory of the origins of the universe is based on the notion that "in the beginning" there was a huge conversion of Energy into Mass—a Big Bang. But what was the source of this tremendous supply of Energy? Christian Realist answer: God? Even more specifically, for John, the *energy* present in the *spoken Word of God*. Although John *eventually* equates this spoken Word with Jesus, at first he is just stating a **Jewish theological concept of the origins of the universe**:

- God is Spirit.
- Spirit is spoken word.
- God's Spirit was the energy source that created the heavens and Earth, originally in their chaotic (formless and void) conditions.
- God's Word/Spirit brought into being all of the order in the universe.

This view is not at odds with a hypothetical Big Bang theory. In fact, this view supplies an important answer for adherents of the Big Bang Theory that physics and Disney's "Universe of Energy" do not supply—the source of the tremendous supply of Energy that was converted into Mass.

Once again, this rhetorical approach to transcending the differing positions of Christian and Scientific Realists is probably not something either the planners of WDW or Disney himself thought through, but the transcendence is possible, through rhetoric.

More photos of the "Universe of Energy" at EPCOT

Chapter 6

Is God MIA at WDW?

Assignment #5: View the fireworks presentation ("Wishes") at the MK. Count the number of nonentities the Disney corporation encourages you to "believe" in—the wishing star, blue fairy, etc. Now, recall the brief one-minute capsule of the origins of the universe, at the "Universe of Energy." Did you see any reference to God, there? Why do you think that is true? What would change, if God were inserted into the sequence?

If, as posited in previous chapters,

- Those who believe the heavens and Earth took a long time to develop need not throw out Judeo-Christian theology, and
- The Big Bang theory of the origins of the universe is not at odds with a Judeo-Christian theology,

why does the "Universe of Energy" exhibit eliminate God from the picture of the origins of the universe?

The MK *does* have a Fantasy Land, something missing from EPCOT. Clearly, the Disney imagineers viewed the MK from a perspective different from their perspective on EPCOT. Peter Pan flies off with you to Never Never Land. You ride a Honey Pot on a blustery day with Winnie the Pooh. You help Seven Dwarfs rescue Snow White from the Quicked Ween, I mean Wicked Queen. So, it's easy enough (with a wink and a nod) to suggest that you should believe in pixie dust, wishes, stars, and fairies.

Yet, there is something eerie about Disney's "Wishes" fireworks presentation. It seems to coalesce closely with Disney's Make-a-Wish Foundation. It hints to children who may have serious or even fatal diseases that there "truly" is **a force in the universe capable of performing miracles**, if they truly believe. What is this force? Apparently, it is something other than God. Why is Disney so hesitant to suggest the equivalent of what the U.S. unabashedly proclaims on its **currency**: "In God we trust"? Disney does not need to protect itself against "**separation of Church and State**" charges; it's a private company. Just outside EPCOT's "American Adventure" in the "World Showcase," during the Christmas season, quite explicit theological accolades are accorded to **Jesus**, every year, in the "**Candlelight Processional**." The "American Adventure" displays the **Declaration of Independence** with its reference to **our Creator**. The "Hall of Presidents" in the MK shows **Abraham Lincoln relying on God** during the Civil War and, again, does not shy away from the Declaration of Independence with its reference to our Creator. Yet, this Creator is strangely absent from EPCOT's account of the origins of the universe in "Universe of Energy."

Blame it on something called "**Occam's Razor**," named for its inventor, **William of Occam**. Occam was an excommunicated English Franciscan thinker from the thirteenth and fourteenth centuries a.d. But, as Burke says, his razor is the "keystone of scientific terminologies." Occam's razor requires that explanations be abbreviated to eliminate any elements science might consider unnecessary to explain how things occur. Kenneth Burke refers to Occam's razor in *Attitudes Toward History*, pages 59 and 166. He explains the Occamite principle in his *Grammar of Motives*, pages 80-81:

> If natural structure was the visible, tangible . . . embodiment of God's will, one would simply be duplicating his terms if his accounts of motivation had both natural and supernatural terms. The natural terms should be enough, in accordance with the Occamite principle (the keystone of scientific terminologies) that "entities should not be multiplied beyond necessity."

(See also *Grammar of Motives* 71, 95, 98, 107, 120, 138, 178, 248, and 324.) I comment on Burke's views concerning Occam on page 53 of *Revelation: The Human Drama*:

> [N]ature is equated with God, as the scene of man's acts, then later God and nature are turned into agonistic terms. What had begun as . . . the view that God created natural laws; hence nature could stand . . . for God . . . developed, due to the Occamite "principle" . . . into the narrowing of a circumference of the scene to simply nature. The "natural" then became contrasted with a no-longer-necessary "supernatural" explanation.

Since the "Universe of Energy" exhibit is based on "scientific terminologies," supernatural terminology is eliminated, in accordance with Occam's razor. God is missing from the story. But, we cannot say that God is MIA (**missing in "action"**), because, without all of the elements of Burke's Pentad—scene, act, agent, agency, purpose—*there is no "action."* There is no Act, if there is no Agent to perform the Act. Occam's razor eliminated the Agent—God. There is no Purpose for the universe, because it takes an Agent to have a Purpose.

THE ISSUE: What is the compelling argument to accept the premise of a William of Occam when the ancient Greek genius Aristotle (with his four causes) and the modern American genius Kenneth Burke (with his Dramatistic Pentad) point out the flaws in such an approach? In my earlier discussion of the *syllogism*, I point out that the syllogism works only if listeners accept the premises. Occam's razor is a premise accepted by Scientific Realists, but believed by Burke and Aristotle to be flawed. So, what would change, if God were inserted into the "Universe of Energy" exhibit? Would the universe again be endowed with meaning? Would humans be more than just the latest step in a continual, unending evolutionary process? Would their symbol-using social nature be an indication of a great purpose of God? Would Walt Disney's motive of building a scene in which families could socialize be comparable to the choice of God to build a scene in which his creatures, made in his image, could socialize with him? Does this seem to be more conducive to living "happily ever after" (a **Disneyesque motive**)?

Photos of the "Wishes" fireworks and Abraham Lincoln in "The Hall of Presidents" at the MK and "The American Adventure" (and, possibly, "The Candlelight Processional") at EPCOT

More Photos

More Photos

Biology

Chapter 7

Which Came First: Plant Life or the Sun?

The ISSUE of this chapter is the **chronological order of creation**. Are there advantages for Christian Realists in the fact that Disney presents a Scientific Realist picture of the origins of the world? One strong advantage may lie in Disney's offering a non-biblical perspective with which to compare any Christian Realist perspectives. The order of Creation in Genesis mirrors the order of the origins of the universe as depicted by Scientific Realists in Disney's EPCOT exhibits. One of those exhibits is no longer present at EPCOT—"The Living Seas" Preshow. Even though it has been removed, the video from the show is still available to anyone who would search "Living Seas Preshow" on the internet. It is worthwhile to watch (a rather poor copy of) this film at: http://www.youtube.com/watch?v=6qdu3qcuzgg

Since the show is in basic agreement with and amplifies the film in the "Universe of Energy," the two shows are collated here to provide a chronology. The following is a chronology supplied by Genesis 1 and EPCOT's "Universe of Energy" and "Living Seas" Preshow exhibits:

- **Gen. 1:2**: "formless and void" mass
- **Disney**: Big Bang

- **Gen. 1:3**: "light"
- **Disney**: "Cloud-covered planet" but "Volcanoes spew"

- **Gen. 1:6**: "the expanse . . . separated the water under the expanse from the water above it"
- **Disney**: "wait and wait and wait . . . until clouds of gasses condense and rain upon the planet"

- **Gen. 1:9**: "Let the water . . . be gathered into . . . seas"
- **Disney**: "rain and rain and rain . . . . the Deluge . . . finally stopped; the Sea had been born"

- **Gen. 1:11**: "Let the land produce vegetation"
- **Disney**: " underwater volcanoes," "small plants . . . single-celled," phytoplankton produce photosynthesis; other vegetation produced chemosynthesis

---

- **Gen. 1:14**: "lights in the expanse of the sky to separate the day from the night, and . . . serve as signs to mark seasons and days and years"
- **Disney**: After the "sea had been born," the sun is now finally visible in "The Living Seas" Preshow film. The same phenomenon is shown in the same order in the "Universe of Energy."

- **Gen. 1:20**: "Let the water teem with living creatures and let birds fly"
- **Disney**: underwater animal life (in "The Living Seas" Preshow) and water-dependent dinosaurs and pterodactyls (in the "Universe of Energy")

- **Gen. 1:24**: "livestock, creatures that move along the ground, and wild animals" followed by "man"
- **Disney**: Other lizards and animals up to and including humans

---

Assignment #6: Recall the sequence of events in the brief one-minute capsule of the origins of the universe in "Universe of Energy." Then, visit "The Seas with Nemo & Friends" attraction at EPCOT. Unfortunately, you will not be able, there, to view what was formerly "The Living Seas" Preshow film. That film has now been replaced with a much less theological Nemo ride.

A further consideration is appropriate here concerning the problem some have with the *introduction by Genesis of the Sun, Moon and stars on Day Four*. Genesis does not say plants were "created" before the sun, moon, and stars. The term "**create**" is used by Genesis only in terms of creating the "heavens and the Earth" in 1:1 (which seems to imply [in the term "heavens"] that the Sun, Moon, and stars may have already been created by Day One), creating "the great creatures of the sea and every living" thing in the sea in 1:21 (the beginning of animal life), and God creating "man in his own image" in 1:27. Genesis states that on the 4th day, the sun, moon, and stars were *made* (visible?) in the firmament, to divide day from night, although Genesis uses the word "**made**" with respect to the heavenly bodies (but not "created"). On the implication of "visibility" in Day 4, lights dividing day from night, being markers for seasons, days, and years, and shedding light upon the Earth seem to strongly imply visibility. This chronological issue of when the Sun, Moon, and stars *came into being* seems to be the major

ISSUE non-believers cite regarding the order of creation in the first chapter of Genesis. Disney's exhibits provide a visual tour of prehistory:

- The Big Bang happens.
- The Earth is hot.
- There is light (from the hot magma and volcanoes?).
- The "waters" are so hot, they are nothing but vapors surrounding the Earth (so dense that no light from the sun, moon, or stars is visible).
- The Earth starts to cool.
- Water vapors begin to condense and gather into seas.
- Vegetation begins.
- Finally, the condensation is so thorough the sun-moon-stars are visible from the surface of the Earth.

One transcendent Christian Realist rhetorical argument relates to the fact that, at some time prior to the sun-moon-stars becoming visible from the surface of the Earth, the Earth's waters were in a gaseous form, hovering above the land surfaces. These water vapors, if they were suspended above the surface of the Earth in gaseous form would be impenetrable by sunlight since, after they condensed and became the sea, one needs only to go below the surface of the sea a few thousand feet before one encounters absolute darkness.

Assignment #7: Now that you have considered the chronological order of creation/origins, do what Christian Realists say God did: take some time to rest and enjoy creation/existence (in chronological order):

Go to the "Land Pavilion" at EPCOT and take the ride "Living with the Land" to enjoy the vegetation. For that matter, just take in all of the scenic landscaping of any Disney park. Enjoy plant life!

View the show "It's Tough to Be a Bug" at the AK to get a glance at really small animal life.

Enjoy the underwater creatures of the "The Seas with Nemo & Friends" exhibit at EPCOT.

Visit the show "Flights of Wonder" at the AK to become better acquainted with the birds of the air. You will see more birds on your safari and walks through "Pangani Forest" and the "Jungle Trek."

Take a jeep ride at "Kilimanjaro Safaris" in the AK to see a wide variety of creeping things (crocodiles), livestock, and wild animals.

When you finish your safari, stroll through "Maharajah Jungle Trek" at the AK. Then see the highest life forms before man—the apes—at "Pangani Forest."

Throughout your visit to WDW, you will encounter the highest creation/being, gathered together from all over the world (and all different cultures): human beings.

Whether or not you believe in God, you might agree with the assessment attributed to God in Genesis 1:3: "God saw all that he had made, and it was very good."

Photos of the scenic landscaping of any Disney park, "The Seas with Nemo & Friends" and "Living with the Land" in EPCOT, "It's Tough to Be a Bug," "Flights of Wonder," "Pangani Forest," the "Maharajah Jungle Trek," and "Kilimanjaro Safaris"at the AK, and humans from all over the world (and all different cultures)

More Photos

Chapter 8

Does Creation Theology Matter?

Assignment #8: Ride through "Spaceship Earth" at EPCOT and notice Disney's rapid presentation of the development of human communication. Beginning with cave drawings (which scholars date no earlier than some 30,000 years ago) humans have found ways to communicate symbolically with one another. Egyptians turned these simple art symbols into a language of hieroglyphics. Phoenicians developed a more universal alphabet. Greeks philosophized, and Romans spread communication through a network of roads.

Creation accounts have been a part of the religious traditions of these ancient cultures and virtually all other cultures since the beginning of recorded history. While some modern Judeo-Christian theologians find it convenient to distance themselves from biblical creation accounts, others question why that is the case. Science is certainly not afraid to tackle issues of the origins of the universe, as has been discussed. Even though the author of Genesis could not have personally known what happened so many years before he was born, there is no reason he should be prohibited from offering an explanation of how the world began. Furthermore, there is room for argumentation that could place the account in Genesis 1 in a context similar to that of current scientific theory.

Virtually **every ancient culture** offered explanations of our origins. The **Egyptians** focused on the role of the *Nile River* in creation. They saw the beginning as a mass of *chaotic waters*, called *Nu* or *Nun*. To this beginning they added *Sun, Moon, Earth, and Sky gods*. The (immortal, but not eternal) Earth god and sky goddess eventually gave birth to *Isis* and *Osiris*, names better known to our generation, but Egyptian mythology (with such features as the Earth god lying on his side to form mountains) did not survive as a serious explanation of the beginnings of the world. According to an account of **Phoenician** creation mythology dating at least as far back as the first century a.d., there was first *chaos*; then from a *cosmic egg*, creation of the universe began. **Mayan** creation stories begin with *sky and sea*, and then the creation god *Kukulkan* (whose pyramid, incidentally, may be seen at the Mexico Pavilion in EPCOT) speaks the word "Earth," and the *Earth* rises from the sea. Following this, the *thoughts* of Kukulkan create *mountains, trees, birds, jaguars,* and *snakes*; finally, *humans* are created (first, out of *mud*; second, out of *wood*; third, as *monkeys*; and finally, as *full-fledged humans*). Vying with Genesis as the oldest creation account is the **Babylonian** creation myth. The Babylonian account we have is developed from **Sumerian** myths, in the 12th century b.c. According to this account, *god/s did not exist at the beginning* of the universe. Instead, *sweet and bitter waters comingled* and created many gods. Then, one god born of two others, *Marduk*, eventually defeated and killed the bitter waters, *Tiamat*, in a colossal struggle. *Earth* was created, followed by the *moon*, then the *Sun*. Finally, *humans* descended from the gods. **Greek** creation mythology began with *chaos*, a watery state ruled by *Oceanus*, and as in the Babylonian account, *reproductive activity on the part of the gods and goddesses* produced the Greek gods. *Poseidon*, one of the great Greek gods (known by the **Romans** as *Neptune*), is featured in a fountain statue in the Italy exhibit in the "World Showcase" at EPCOT.

Of all ancient explanations of the origins of the universe, only the **Hebrew** account has withstood the test of time. Only the Hebrew account has continued throughout years of

Modernism and **Postmodernism** to survive the vast onslaught of *scientific skepticism* and Postmodern *relativism*. Even so, the Hebrew account of world origins remains under severe attack and is strongly derided by many. THE ISSUE: *Should Christian Realists bother to fight this battle?* This issue is important; it goes to the very heart of keeping the terms "**creator**" and "omnipotent" in definitions of God. How could the world and everything in it be the product of an **omnipotent agent**, if there is no agent capable of creating the world? Without an Agent, would the world have any **Purpose**? How could any hope of an "**afterlife**" be placed in God, if he was not even capable of creating the "present" life? If there is no afterlife, not only the descriptive terms "omnipotent" and "creator" but also the terms "**eternal**" and "**immutable**" should be removed from one's definition of God. If God did not create the universe, how could anyone claim that he is "**omnipresent**" in it? If he is not omnipresent, how could he possibly know all things (be "**omniscient**") about it? In short, what happens to the entire definition of God from Chapter 2, if one applies *Occam's Razor* to creation?

If God is not omnipotent, eternal, immutable, omnipresent, and omniscient, should people assume that no one is and that the humans we call geniuses are at the *top of the ladder*, when it comes to approximations concerning these characteristics? Not all **evolutionists** are willing to go there. Some believe that, since there is **"intelligent" life** on Earth, logic demands that there must be "even more intelligent" life elsewhere in the universe. The argument is that there must be **aliens** who are more intelligent (-scient), aliens who are more powerful (-potent), aliens who can extend their lives further (approximating eternity), etc. Do we have any clear proof of the existence of such aliens?

Compare the intelligent alien theory with the Hebrew account of the existence of a God who created the universe, written thousands of years ago, positing a more intelligent, powerful, eternal being, capable of creating the entire universe. Both posit the existence of intelligent life beyond the Earth. Does either account stand in close agreement with the best scientific evidence available concerning the *chronological order of the origins of the universe*? Does either account supply the *missing link that the Big Bang theory does not*: Where did the energy to produce the

Big Bang come from? Does either account supply a *dramatistic explanation for human existence* (based on Burke's Pentad)? Does either *employ Occam's Razor as science does*? Since humans seem to be hard-wired with a *dramatistic nature*, does either explain why we have that nature? And, since humans have the capacity to be intelligent, powerful, and creative life-extenders, *does the existence of the human species argue* for the existence of God, a being with even greater supplies of these same characteristics, or for the likelihood of intelligent alien beings? Is there *something built into the human psyche* that seems to cry out: "God created the heavens and the Earth"? If so, is that why "creation accounts have been a part of the religious traditions of . . . virtually all cultures since the beginning of recorded history"?

Many other ancient religious traditions of creation have fallen by the wayside, because they contained clearly erroneous stories. The Hebrew author of the Genesis 1 account, living thousands of years ago, at least provided a provocative account of the origins of the universe. On pages 95-96 of *Psychotic Entelechy: The Dangers of Spiritual Gifts Theology*, the following obvious observation is offered:

> Genesis provides a rapid-fire account of more than two thousand years of human
> history prior to Israel's four hundred year sojourn in Egypt. Prior to the account
> of human history, Genesis offers a one-chapter account of the creation of heaven,
> Earth, and the plant and animal kingdoms. Presumably, if Moses authored the
> creation and human history accounts, he would need some inspiration from God
> to certify that his account was accurate.

Whether or not an account of creation theology from a given religion has persuasive power, it is clear that religions throughout history have found it important to practice religious rhetoric in the area of creation theology. Religious rhetoric at WDW raises the issue. Because of the conflict between Disney's Christian Realist tendencies and his Scientific Realist tendencies, the Hebrew account has been highlighted in this chapter, but the creation rhetoric of other religions (such as Mayan, Greek and Roman religions) is also implicit in the religious symbolism of WDW.

Photos of (the various cultures at) "Spaceship Earth" in EPCOT

More Photos

Chapter 9

What about Evolution?

Assignment #9: Catch a meal at the "Sci-Fi Dine In" restaurant at HS. Study the aliens. Do you notice any signs of an implicit belief in evolution? Ride the "Great Movie Ride" at the HS. Pay attention to the movie trailers from "*Alien*" and "*Fantasia*" (specifically, "The Rite of Spring") and see if you see any "powerful" alien creatures in the "*Alien*" set you ride through. Join "Stitch's Great Escape" in the MK. Walk through "Pangani Forest" of the AK. Is there any evolutionary rhetoric to be found?

The most stressful and emotionally divisive debate between Scientific Realists and Christian Realists is over the ISSUE of **evolution**. Walt Disney was certainly familiar with the Scopes Trial of 1925. Does WDW address the issue? *Conservatives* (who may have even misinterpreted fellow conservatives' positions on this issue) consign fellow conservatives to Satan because they think the others do not totally agree with them. *Liberals* dismiss as silly anyone who is not a "true believer" in **Darwinism** (something that is far from being proven, itself). The entire discussion gets rather mean-spirited, at times. The objective of this chapter is to give fair consideration to all sides of the Christian Realist and Scientific Realist issue, to help people wrestle with their own views.

The last chapter mentioned evolutionists who believed that logically, there must be more intelligent life on other planets. The "logic" of this belief is expressed in the **Drake Equation**, developed by Frank Drake, in 1961: $N = R_* f_p n_e f_l f_i f_c L$. The name of this "branch of science" (that has produced no empirical evidence of any kind of life on other planets) is "astrobiology." A famous popularizer of extraterrestrial intelligent life theory and astronomy, **Carl Sagan**, came up with a plan for attaching some sort of message to U.S. spacecraft that may be destined to leave the Earth permanently. Sagan was not thinking some extraterrestrial "plant" would be able to decipher his message. Sagan's hope was that his message might eventually be interpreted by some **extraterrestrial intelligent life** form that might find our spacecraft. Some of Sagan's notions are dramatized in the 1997 movie, *Contact*. These ideas were clearly floating around before Sagan and Drake became famous. Disney producers were already toying with the relationship between evolutionary theories and extraterrestrial life in the 1950s.

On December 4, 1957, the *Disneyland* television series on ABC TV aired an episode entitled "Mars and Beyond," directed by **Ward Kimball**. The episode is included in a *Walt Disney Treasures* collection entitled *Tomorrowland: Disney in Space and Beyond*, available through online channels. Film critic **Ernest Rister** (http://dvd.ign.com/articles/518/518352p1.html) explains:

> [The episode offers] the history of evolution on Earth (creationists, beware) in a sequence that strongly echoes the "Rite of Spring" sequence from Fantasia, without re-using any of the 1940 animation. Then we are shown how life may have evolved on other planets in a bravura animated set-piece that is as strong as anything to come out of the Disney studios in the 1950s.

This piece of **textual evidence** may be important proof that Walt Disney believed in evolution, but does that mean he rejected creation theology? Even if Disney accepted evolution as an explanation of the origin and development of life on Earth, has evolution been scientifically proven? Scientific Realist believers in gradual evolution have been hoping that the study of fossils (**paleontology**) will yield scientific evidence of the various transitional stages of development each genus and species went through as it evolved. They are searching for "**missing links**." The website AllAboutScience.org (http://www.allaboutscience.org/missing-link-faq.htm) reports:

> Stephen J. Gould, America's most famous evolutionist . . . stated, "The extreme rarity of transitional forms in the fossil record persists as the trade secret of paleontology. The evolutionary . . . textbooks have data only at the tips and nodes of their branches; the rest is inference, however reasonable, not the evidence of fossils. I wish in no way to impugn the potential validity of gradualism. I wish only to point out that it was never seen in the rocks."

Gould's comments may be used by Christian Realists who wish to reject concepts of evolution altogether. Such Christian Realists may insist that "the extreme rarity of transitional forms in the **fossil record**" may be taken as proof that **gradualism** (evolution) did not occur. Such a view may be supported by the biblical creation account, which uses the phrase "according to its/their kind/s" throughout creation (Genesis 1:11, 21, 24, 25). This "kind/s" terminology may indicate a doctrine of the existence of biological boundaries that are not crossed by evolution. Hence, there would necessarily be missing links. Nevertheless, there are other Christian Realists who are persuaded that some evolution/gradualism did occur. Does the biblical creation account rule out any possibility of evolution/gradualism?

The ISSUE (for Christian Realists) is *"how" God created and/or made things*. Genesis 2:8 states that God had "planted" a garden in Eden, but this is surely not an indication of how God made plants. Planting presupposes that one has seeds to plant. Given the existence of seeds, even humans can "plant" a garden. Did God form each plant or seed that grew? Perhaps, but Genesis does not make that claim.

Genesis 1:11 indicates "how" God made plants. He *spoke* to the land: "Let the land produce vegetation." Genesis 1:12 confirms: "The land produced vegetation." One way of viewing this phenomenon is to say that God *delegated* to land the capacity for producing plant life. If land, then, was given by God the capacity to produce life, one should not be terribly surprised if, at some point, humans—putting together the right combination of chemicals from the land—are able to see that "land" (i.e., a chemical combination) produce life (in a test tube, for example). My high school science teacher predicted to me nearly a half century ago that we were on the verge of such an accomplishment. However, it has not happened yet.

In a somewhat similar manner (but with a curious departure in the way it is phrased), in Genesis 1:20, God *spoke* to the waters: "Let the waters teem with living creatures." Did God, then, according to Genesis, endow the waters with the capacity to produce animal life? Possibly. Possibly not. Note that, in Genesis 1:21, "God created . . . every living and moving thing with which the water teems." This seems to be a special act (hence, the use of the word "created"). Water animal life was the first level of animal life. As noted before, there are just a few times Genesis employs the term "create" in the creation account. This is one of them.

Genesis 1:24 returns to a formula similar to the formula for making plants. God *spoke* to the land: "Let the land produce living creatures." If God delegated to land the capacity for producing plant life, and then (later) the capacity for producing living creatures, it may be argued that once God created elemental animal life (in the waters), the land was given the capacity for developing that animal life. In other words, there appears to be some room for a somewhat **biblically-based evolution/gradualism theory**.

Note, however, that Genesis once again employs the term "create" when it comes to humans. Genesis 1:27 states: "God created man in his own image . . . male and female created He them." Genesis 2:7 adds the detail that God formed man from the dust of the ground and breathed into his nostrils the breath of life before man became a living being. As previously mentioned, "the term 'create' is used by Genesis only in terms of creating the 'heavens and the Earth' in 1:1 . . . creating 'the great creatures of the sea and every living' thing in the sea in 1:21 (the beginning of animal life), and God creating 'man in his own image' in 1:27." Nevertheless, according to Genesis, all creation seems to have been accomplished by God "speaking," with the lone exception of the creation of Adam. Those Christian Realists who wish to accommodate some form of evolution/gradualism theory in their theology would do well to pay attention to the significant shifts of these three "create" events.

Regardless of whether Christian Realists choose to reject evolution altogether or to accommodate some elements of evolutionary theory in their theologies, a motto borrowed from the Restoration Movement could be useful in reducing the theological community stress over this issue. I refer to the motto on page 36 of *The Seven Cs of Stress*:

> There was a nineteenth century motto promoting church unity, which suggested: "In essentials, unity. In opinions, liberty. In all things, love." The second element of that catch phrase is a principle of **anarchy**. There may be instances in which each individual should have the latitude to decide for himself or herself. When there is no compelling reason for everyone in the group to be doing the same thing, why not provide liberty/anarchy?

Is there a compelling reason for every Christian Realist to hold exactly the same view regarding the evolution issue? When **Martin Luther** debated the Catholic Church over **The Ninety-Five Theses**, he tried to establish the compelling basis upon which *he* thought all Christians could find unity: *Sola Scriptura* (the Bible alone). If a Christian Realist cites a plausible biblically-based argument for the opinion s/he holds, it may be a situation that cries out for liberty (for those who argue for biblical positions).

I recently asked a cast member at the AK where in the park I could find references to evolution. She answered that she did not know of any. (That does not mean that none exist, however.) Perhaps, the Disney imagineers considered this issue to be too controversial. Nevertheless, Disney opens the door to such a rhetorical exercise by airing the *Disneyland* television episode "Mars and Beyond," if nothing else.

Photos of the "Sci-Fi Dine In" restaurant and the "Great Movie Ride" at HS, "Stitch's Great Escape" at MK, and "Pangani Forest" at AK

Anthropology

Chapter 10

How Does One Make an Invisible Image?

Assignment #10: Ride the "Great Movie Ride" in HS and pay special attention to the Indiana Jones set where Indy is moving the Ark of the Covenant. Notice that on top of the Ark are two golden angels with their wings touching in the middle of the Ark. The place where the wings meet is called the "Mercy Seat." Hebrew theology says that God sits above that seat. Look very carefully above the seat. Do you see anything?

In Chapters 2, 3, and 8, the famous theological descriptive terms—omniscient, omnipotent, eternal, omnipresent, and immutable are considered. Kenneth Burke, in *The Rhetoric of Religion*, page 22, discusses what he calls:

> "**Negative theology**," the defining of God in terms of what he is not, as when God is described in words like "immortal," "immutable," "infinite," "unbounded," impassive," and the like . . . since God, by being "supernatural," is not describable by the positives of nature."

Logically speaking, a God who created nature cannot be restricted to the laws of nature. Another negative term Judaism adds to the description of God is "**invisible**." The Ark of the Covenant (as presented visually in the movie *Raiders of the Lost Ark*) was designed to symbolically make this point.

All other gods presented at WDW are **visible**. The Hebrew God is invisible. Notice the following gods at WDW, for example:

- **Gaia** is encountered when you are greeted by some cast members in the AK. They may say, or you may also see a sign when approaching the Tree of Life that says "Viva Gaia!" Viva Gaia means "Long live Gaia!" There is no statue of this ancient Greek goddess because you are standing on her. Gaia is *the Earth goddess*.

- **Pegasus**, the *Greek Horse god*, is encountered in the "Great Movie Ride" (in the film clip from *Fantasia*) at HS. Pegasus is the horse with wings.

- **Kukulkan**, the *Mayan creation god*, may be seen at the Mexico Pavilion in EPCOT. He is the feathery serpent whose head protrudes multiple times from the columns that ascend the pyramid. As previously mentioned, **Mayan** creation stories begin with sky and sea, and then the creation god Kukulkan speaks the word "Earth," and the Earth rises from the sea.

- The *Roman god of the sea*, **Neptune** (also known as the *Greek god* **Poseidon**), may be seen in the Italy pavilion at EPCOT. If you are familiar with the Disney film, *The Little Mermaid*, you will know that the little mermaid's father is King Triton. **Triton** is the *sea messenger god, the son of Poseidon*. In other accounts of the little mermaid, her father is Neptune himself. **Hans Christian Anderson**, who wrote down the fairy tale, identifies the father only as "the Sea King."

- The **stone god and other Egyptian gods** you saw in the Raiders of the Lost Ark set as you rode the Great Movie Ride at HS are also quite visible.

- Shane Lindsay adds: "Also check the ceiling in the main rotunda where you purchase rounds for Fantasia MiniGolf. You'll see a giant blue image of **Zeus** smiling down at you from the clouds. It's actually quite evocative of the Sistine Ceiling."

While visiting Norway, China, and Japan in EPCOT's "World Showcase," you may notice **other visible gods** (or, at least, the images of these gods).

In virtually all ages and cultures, humans have **worshiped the images** of their gods. This fact presented a particular theological problem for the Hebrews. Their God was invisible, as Burke said: "'**supernatural**,' . . . not describable by the positives of nature." They reasoned that a God who created nature cannot be restricted to the laws of nature. Therefore, one way they depicted this invisible God was with the Ark of the Covenant. The Ark was a chest that was believed to originally contain the two stone tablets with the engraving of the Ten Commandments. On the top of the Ark were images of two **cherubim** whose wings met above the middle of the Ark. There, above the meeting of these wings is where the "invisible" God was seated. Hence, God was the invisible being that hierarchically ranked above the cherubim and was represented in the Ark by his most significant message to his People, the **Ten Commandments**. In the film clip in the preview to The Great Movie Ride, the Ark is called "a transmitter, a radio for speaking to God." The Ark represented not only God's invisible nature, it represented his nature as a communicator.

Human Symbolicity as Divine Image

That is *one way* to make an invisible image. The *other way* involves a theology that is not as well-known. It involves the Genesis teaching that God made man into his "image." I describe some of the significance of this theology in *Revelation: The Human Drama*. Revelation describes a Beast (whom the vast majority of Revelation scholars interpret as first century Rome). Then, Revelation says that the inhabitants of the land were forced to make an **"image" of this Beast** and to worship this image. Agreeing with two of the most important Revelation scholars of the past two centuries, I point out that the image of the Beast is a sort of person within a person. The image is not a stone or silver or gold image; it is a "human"—the Jewish High Priest in the late first century a.d. Just as Adam was the "image" of God, so also is the image of the Beast a human. In Revelation, Jesus (like a second Adam) is the image of God and is set in contrast to the image of the Beast. Worshipers in Revelation are encouraged in Chapters 4 and 5 to worship both God and the Lamb.

This may be a bit too arcane for the reader, but perhaps, the following quotation from page 88 of my book on Revelation will clarify this point:

> If, as Wellhausen claims, "[The image of the Beast] is the alter ego of the empire just as Jesus was called the [image] of God" (cf. II Corinthians 4:4 and Colossians 1:15), then a living human being serves as the "image" of the beast, just as the human, Jesus, serves as the "image" of God. Where exactly Wellhausen derives his information that Jesus is the [image] of God, Charles does not indicate; and the explicit statement is found nowhere in Revelation. However, [in a Jewish book written between the end of the Old Testament and the beginning of the New Testament] *Vita Adae et Evae* 13-14 . . . clearly calls Adam the "image" of God [and, therefore, has God requiring angels to worship Adam], and [Jewish scholar Louis] Ginzberg sees in . . . [Hebrews 1:6] the link which makes Jesus a second Adam in the fashion of *Vita*, hence making him worthy of worship. Thus . . . literature with which John could easily be familiar has a human serving as an "image," and therefore receiving "worship."

> If John is making the "image" of God (Jesus) in Revelation 5 "worthy of praise," then, in antithetical fashion, he could be making the "image" of the beast (the high priest) in Revelation 13 the object of (unworthy) antichristian worship. . . . Instead of an image of stone, the Jews had in the middle of their temple an amazing sign--an image that could "speak" (13:15)! He was the voice of the Empire in the midst of the temple.

How can a human be the "image" of an invisible God when humans are clearly visible? The religious rhetoric argues that there is an invisible characteristic of humans that is the "image" of God, while the visible characteristics of humans are *not* the image of God. Kenneth Burke claims that humans have two characteristics—**animality** and **symbolicity**. Our animality would be the *physical characteristics of humans* (similar to other animals). Our symbolicity would be that *invisible characteristic that makes us different from all other animals*. We communicate by using what Burke calls "**symbols**," while all other animals communicate by what Burke calls "**signals**." Burke calls man "**the symbol-using animal**." The dedication to *Implicit Rhetoric: Kenneth Burke's Extension of Aristotle's Concept of Entelechy* reads: "To God, the Ultimate Symbol-User." The implication is that this "symbol-using" nature of both God and humans could be taken, rhetorically, to be the image of God into which humans were made. The next few chapters will explore this ISSUE in more detail.

Photos of the Ark of the Covenant in the "Great Movie Ride" and "Voyage of The Little Mermaid" at HS, the "Viva Gaia!" sign in the AK, Kukulkan at the Mexico Pavilion, Neptune (a.k.a. Poseidon) at the Italy pavilion, and Norway, China, and Japan's other visible gods at EPCOT, and Zeus at the Fantasia MiniGolf.

More photos

Chapter 11

Man's Symbolicity=God's Image?

Assignment #11: Ride "Spaceship Earth" at EPCOT. This time, you are looking for symbol-use. What symbols are used in the cave drawings, hieroglyphics, sculpture, chapel artwork, movies, television, etc.?

The centerpiece in all of Walt Disney World for the study of human communication is "Spaceship Earth." Visitors journey through the **history of human communication**. *Cave drawings, hieroglyphics, papyrus scrolls, Phoenician alphabet, Greek philosophy, Roman roads, the Dark Ages, Jewish scribes, Islamic scholars, Christian monks, moveable type, the Renaissance, sculpture and chapel artwork, newspapers, telegraph, telephone, movies, radio, television,* and finally, *the computer age.* The entire history of human communication exemplifies the **definition of humans** offered by Kenneth Burke on page 16 of *Language as Symbolic Action*:

> Man is the symbol-using (symbol-making, symbol-misusing) . . . animal, inventor
> of (and moralized by) the negative . . . separated from his natural condition by

instruments of his own making, goaded by the spirit of hierarchy (or moved by a sense of order) . . . and rotten with perfection.

Take out the word "animal," and this definition of human approximates a definition of God. In the next few chapters, we will compare Burke's definition, phrase by phrase. This chapter just explores the first phrase.

Phrase 1: Symbol-Using (Symbol-Making). The **first attribute** of a symbol is that a **symbol** is something that *stands for or represents something else*. As Korzybski observed, "The word 'tree' is not a tree." Yet, the word "tree" represents or stands for a real tree. The word "tree" is therefore a symbol. Nevertheless, the word "tree" is not the *only* symbol for a real tree. If you were German, the word "*baum*" would be your symbol for a real tree (as you may remember from the Christmas song, O Tannen-*baum*.) The French, Spanish, Italians, Greeks, Hebrews, Chinese, Japanese, Portuguese, Russians, etc. all use different symbols for the same real tree. If you were a **caveman**, the symbol for a real tree would be a drawing of a tree on the cave wall. If you used **hieroglyphics**, the symbol would resemble a tree. According to http://www.virtual-egypt.com/html/hieroglyphics.htm, "There were basically 604 symbols that might be put to [use] . . . as an ideogram, as when a sign resembling a tree meant 'tree.'" The **Phoenicians** developed an **alphabet**, which most western civilizations use to this day. They created symbols (letters) to represent each sound, so t, r, e, and e, when combined, help us sound out the word "tree." These letters are symbols, but they are not the *only* symbols for sounds. Greek letters are somewhat different from Phoenician letters, but represent similar sounds. Hebrew, Arabic, Chinese, and Japanese letters are much different, but still help humans sound out words. **Sign language** provides symbols for those who may not even be able to sound out words. **Braille** provides symbols for those who cannot see.

Why do humans have so many symbols for the same thing? Why can we not automatically understand the messages of other humans, from any part of the globe? **Other animals** have no such problem, so far as we know. Whales from the North Atlantic seem to be able to understand the communication of whales from the South Pacific. Japanese dogs seem to understand the barks of American Beagles. Bees understand the messages of the flight patterns of other bees, even though they have had no time to learn the meanings. It is because animals communicate with "signals," not "symbols." A signal is "programmed communication." The animal **instinctively** knows the meaning of the communication of its own species. Humans have a different form of communication. As Burke observes, humans *make* their symbols.

The symbol does not even need to make sense. The **second attribute** of a symbol is that it may be *arbitrarily chosen*. Some words, such as the "hiss" of a snake appear to have been *logically created*. Other words may appear to *make no sense whatsoever*, as when I tell my students that my word for chalk is "bleh." Yet, after having heard me say that, if I ask someone to hand me some bleh, that student hands me a piece of chalk. It may seem simple to draw a picture of a tree. But, what other animal has ever drawn even something so simple as a picture? Our cave-dwelling human ancestors did, however. Theologically, you could say that "symbol-making" is a *creative* act. The very fact that humans *create* their own forms of communication argues rhetorically that humans have a god-like nature. They may be said, in that sense, to be "in the image of God," if we define God as *Creator*.

So, who decides which symbol we should use when referring to a tree? The **third attribute** of a symbol is that *there must be shared meaning*. English speakers are able to read this book, but those who know only another language cannot. Not even all English speakers know what I mean when I use words like "arbitrary," "immutable," etc. But, now that you know the word "bleh," we have shared meaning. I can ask you to mail me some and you would at least understand my request. At times, we need to *limit our vocabulary* use to those words with which our audience is familiar—even if it means that *we must be less precise* in our communication.

Enter theology. One problem God may, theoretically, have had in communicating to humans thousands of years ago is their **limited vocabulary**. I discussed in an earlier chapter that Genesis uses the word "*yom*" or "day" in a variety of different ways. Perhaps, that is because the audience of Genesis had a limited vocabulary. One word had to do yeoman's service. Wait! Did everyone understand the word "yeoman"? Or, did you have to look it up? This does not mean that God as a symbol-user does not know what he wants to communicate. It may mean that his audience does not have shared meaning with the terms/symbols he could use. How could the original audience of Genesis have possibly understood symbols like "the curvature of space time" or "$E=MC^2$"? Those who are quick to criticize the scientific teachings of Genesis should at least consider that communication with humans is limited by the amount of shared meaning possible in any context.

Photos of (the various examples of symbol-use at) "Spaceship Earth" in EPCOT

Chapter 12

Man's Morality=God's Image?

Assignment #12: Visit virtually any Disney attraction ("The Haunted Mansion" at the MK, for example). List the "Thou shalt not's" you are confronted with: Thou shalt not take flash photography, eat, drink, smoke, ride if you are not at least this height or under this age, use cell phones, place your hands outside your vehicle, stand up, sit down, put on your 3-D glasses until instructed to, etc. Disney has its own version of the Ten Commandments pertaining to each ride. Have a snack at (or just a visit to) Pinocchio's Village Haus restaurant in the MK. Surrounded by a scene resembling that of Disney's movie, think of the implicit "Thou shalt not's" in the movie, *Pinocchio*: Thou shalt not be truant, drink, smoke, or play pool.

The previous chapter considered the first phrase of Kenneth Burke's definition of human: "symbol-using, symbol-making." It suggested that symbolicity was one way in which humans are the image of God. This chapter considers the second phrase, which depends on the first phrase for its existence. The entire definition, again, is:

Man is the symbol-using (symbol-making, symbol-misusing) . . . animal, inventor of (and moralized by) the negative . . . separated from his natural condition by instruments of his own making, goaded by the spirit of hierarchy (or moved by a sense of order) . . . and rotten with perfection.

Phrase 2: Inventor of (and Moralized by) the Negative. This phrase, like the first phrase applies to both humans and God.   Even though, theoretically, God, like humans, uses symbols or words, he uses two types of words. Burke calls the **first type**--words he uses in creating the world (**capitalized**) "**Word**."   If God speaks a "Word," that Word has "*omnipotence*" (or, at least, the total power necessary to complete its task). In Genesis 1:3, God speaks a Word ("And God said, 'Let there be light'"). The very Word he speaks has the "omnipotence" to produce light. Psalms 33:9 confirms the power of this (capitalized) Word: "He spoke, and it was done; he commanded, and [the universe] stood fast." The Word of God has tremendous power. Isaiah 55:11 goes so far as to suggest that God's Word is *infallible*--it cannot fail: "So is my word that goes out from my mouth; it will not return to me empty, but will accomplish what I desire and achieve the purpose for which I sent it."

How, then, can God give a command (word) to Adam and Eve not to eat of the Tree of Knowledge of Good and Evil, and have that word *fail* to achieve its purpose? How is it possible that after the command from God was issued, Adam and Eve ate anyway? The **second type** of word God uses is (**lower-case**) "**word**." Burke offers theological distinctions between "word" and "Word." This (lower-case) "word" has much less power to affect humans. Burke identifies the *basis upon which he distinguishes between the two types of words*--**the negative**.

The negative is an interesting concept. The symbol "tree" is a symbol for something that positively exists, but what is "not a tree"? Animals may, through classical conditioning, even understand our "positive" symbols. But, the negative is *a "symbol" for the absence of something*. Animals may conceive of "food," but they cannot conceive of "not food." My dog, Nicolete, grew up with my daughter's dog, Pigeon. If I say the word "Pigeon," Nicolete perks up and looks around to find her.   If I say, "No, Nicolete, Pigeon is not here," Nicolete becomes even more intent on finding her. She does not understand the negative. Similarly, she likes to take a "walk." She runs to the door and waits. If I say, "Sorry, I do not have time for a walk," she happily jumps around at the door. She knows only what the positive word "walk" means; she does not understand what the negative "not walk" means. Burke, however, is most interested in what he calls the *hortatory* negative, the negative of command, as with the "Thou shalt not's" of the Ten Commandments.

Clearly implied in any "Thou shalt not" is the **element of free will** or **choice**. We do *not* tell anyone "Thou shalt not" do something it is *impossible* to not do. It does no good to tell a baby not to cry. We do not tell people not to digest the food in their intestines. We do not tell someone not to let his or her heart beat, hair or fingernails grow, or kidneys work. We do not use such hortatory negatives because people have no choice in such matters. On the other hand, if we tell people, "Thou shalt not kill, lie, steal, rape, commit adultery, or slander," it is clear that humans have free will or choice in such matters. They may choose either to kill or to not kill. They may choose to lie or to tell the truth. They may choose to steal or to refrain from stealing, to rape or refrain from raping, to commit adultery or to refrain from committing adultery, to slander or not to slander. Having this distinction in mind, I should point out that, although God's utterance is presented as "Word" in the case of the creative fiat ("Let there be light!"), God's utterance might be understood as "word" in the case of the Ten Commandments. In the first instance, there is no implicit free will attributed to that which is created. In the second instance, humans to whom the Ten Commandments are directed are implicitly credited with free will. If God extends free will and choice to humans by issuing hortatory negatives, or (lower case) word, God has just made humans into "free moral agents." Another way of putting this is to say that God has made "man into his image." Just as God is free to do whatever he wants to do, by issuing hortatory negatives, God has made man free. He is an "agent," just as God is an agent.

Burke defines man as "*moralized* by the negative." Animals, since they are not "symbol-users," and therefore cannot understand the hortatory negative, do not have morality. Whatever they do is prescribed by *instinct* and *classical conditioning*. "Thou shalt not" is the basis of all morality.

While I may tell my dog, "No," she does not interpret the negative as a negative. She interprets the word as a positive command to stop in her tracks. She learns that, if she does not stop, she will experience pain; if she does stop, she may experience pleasure (a treat). This is classical (or operant) conditioning. Jewish theology, on the other hand, suggests that humans have both a **good inclination** and an **evil inclination**; humans are capable of choosing to do either good or evil. When humans have the option to do either good or evil and yet *choose* to do good, they are the image of a God who, according to Christian Realists, chooses good over evil 100% of the time.

Photos of Pinocchio's Village Haus Restaurant in the MK

Chapter 13

Man's Tool-Making=God's Image?

Assignment #13: Journey on the "Jungle Cruise" at the MK. Pay close attention to depictions of the natives. List any tools they are carrying, especially tools for hunting.

Now that we have considered the first two phrases of Kenneth Burke's definition of human--"symbol-using, symbol-making" and "inventor of (and moralized by) the negative"--we turn to the third phrase.

Phrase 3: Separated from His Natural Condition by Instruments of His Own Making. God, as the creator of nature, would *not* have a "natural" condition. He would be **"super"-natural** (above nature). In the sense of being "separated from his natural condition by instruments of his own making," one could also say that *man is "super"-natural*. Animals may "adapt" to their natural environment through mutation, but humans can separate themselves from the limitations of their natural environment by symbol-use. Humans, using symbolic logic, are able to "make" instruments that remove the limitations of nature. If humans live in a cold environment, they "make" clothing, insulated homes, fireplaces, central heat, thermal underwear, etc. If humans live in a hot environment, they "make" electric fans, backyard swimming pools, central air conditioning, etc. If humans desire to travel faster than their legs can "naturally" carry them, they make chariots, bicycles, automobiles, motorboats, airplanes, jets, etc. If they, like other animals, are Earth-bound as a part of their natural condition, they make rockets and space shuttles. Chapter 3 of *Implicit Rhetoric: Kenneth Burke's Extension of Aristotle's Concept of Entelechy*, is entitled "The Human as Super-Natural." The human is the only animal to have the ability to transcend natural limitations by his rational thought, symbol-use, and inventions.

Consider the human natives you encounter along the "Jungle Cruise" route. Even uncivilized cultures knew how to be super-natural (to separate themselves from their natural condition by instruments of their own making). It is true that *sea otters* can "use" tools (that they do not make). They can "find" rocks and use the rocks as tools to break open the shells of shellfish, so they can eat the meat inside. It is true that *apes* will use sticks they "find" to place in holes and crevices to retrieve insects and other foods. However, the sea otters and apes do not "make" these instruments—they "find" them in their natural environment. Humans, on the other hand, "make" the instruments that separate them from their natural condition.

While sea otters may "use" rocks as tools, humans "make" the rocks into cutting instruments. They chip away edges of the rocks to make sharp **knives**. Humans did this—even in the *Stone Age*. Then, humans realized that they could use vines to tie their sharp rocks to sticks and they "made" **axes**. The humans, next, realized they could put the sharpened rocks on the ends of longer sticks, so they did not have to come into close contact with the animals they hunted. They had invented **spears**. They noticed they could throw these spears, but if they tied vines to each end of a willow stick and bent the stick, they could use this bow to propel smaller spears (arrows). Every single human culture, it seems, has learned to "make" **bows and arrows**. But, it did not stop there.

When riding through "Spaceship Earth," you noticed all of the **tools for saving and sending** (via the media) the **pieces of symbolic communication** the humans had "made": *stone tablets, papyrus, chisels, pens, paint brushes, moveable type, printing presses, newspapers, telegraph,* *telephone*, *radio*, *motion pictures*, *television*, and *computers*.   When riding through the "Universe of Energy," you saw the humorous slice-of-life demonstrating that humans learned to **control fire** (something no other animal has learned) and found that the use of that basic form of energy led to other **tools for using energy**: *steam engines*, *internal combustible engines*, *hydroelectric dams*, *solar energy collectors*, *oil wells*, *off-shore drilling platforms*, *windmills*, and *nuclear power plants*.

Yet, with all of this tool-making by humans, no other animal has figured out how to make its own rudimentary stone knife. Humans are the super-natural animal. Hence, you could say that they are the "image" of God.

Assignment #14: Since you have considered the tool-making nature of human beings, explore the celebration of some of those inventions. Ride "The Walt Disney World Railroad" at the MK, then the "Monorail" to EPCOT, then "Test Track" at EPCOT (but pay attention to all of the tests of the automobile you see in the queue leading up to the ride). Next, ride "Soarin'" and "Mission Space," to feel what it is like to fly and space travel. (CAUTION: unless you have a really strong stomach and are resistant to dizziness, the milder version of the "mission space" ride or not riding at all is recommended.) Since you are traveling into space, you may want to ride "Star Tours" in HS, and join R2-D2 in a (futuristic) space mission.

Photos of the "Jungle Cruise" and "The Walt Disney World Railroad" at the MK, the "Monorail" to EPCOT, "Test Track," "Soarin'," and "Mission Space" at EPCOT, and "Star Tours" in HS

More Photos

Chapter 14

Man's Symbolic Hierarchies=God's Image?

Assignment #15: Ride "The Great Movie Ride" in HS. Notice the chimney sweeps in the Mary Poppins scene and consider the line of the song "Chim Chim Cheree" that states: "Now as the ladder of life 'as been strung, you may think a sweep's on the bottommost rung." What does that song say about hierarchy? Visit the gorillas in "Pangani Forest" in the AK. Which gorilla do you believe is at the top of the gorilla hierarchy in that collection of gorillas? Now, visit "The Hall of Presidents" in the MK. Clearly, presidents are the top of the hierarchy in the U.S., but do you detect any hierarchy among the various presidents (a top of the top), according to the Disney presentation?

Recall that we are still considering Kenneth Burke's definition of human:

> Man is the symbol-using (symbol-making, symbol-misusing) . . . animal, inventor
> of (and moralized by) the negative . . . separated from his natural condition
> by instruments of his own making, goaded by the spirit of hierarchy (or moved by
> a sense of order) . . . and rotten with perfection.

We have considered three phrases and are now ready for **Phrase 4: Goaded by the Spirit of Hierarchy (Or Moved by a Sense of Order)**.

Virtually all animals have hierarchies, but (other than humans) these hierarchies are all **"natural" hierarchies**. In the insect world (which you visited in the show "It's Tough to be a Bug" in the AK), the top of the hierarchy is typically a female, such as the **Queen Bee**. Among such birds as chickens, there is a "**pecking order**." One chicken (or rooster) is in a position in which s/he has earned the honor of not being "peckable" by other fowl. (This is not the same as when English speakers speak "impeccable" German!) This non-peckable chicken is allowed to peck every other chicken in the hen-yard. However, none of the others can peck her/him. There are those below this chicken who can peck every other chicken *except* the one at the top of the hierarchy. And, so it goes until you reach that one chicken that is peckable by every other chicken in the hen-yard, but is not allowed to peck *any* other chicken back. We call that lowest one on the hierarchy "hen-pecked." Humans, noticing this natural hierarchy, label husbands who do not seem capable of fighting back against their wives' onslaughts "henpecked." A similar phenomenon occurs among wolves. The "leader of the pack" is allowed to bite the back of every other member of the wolf-pack. Some lowly wolf is bitten by all the pack, but cannot bite any other wolf. Humans, noticing this natural hierarchy, speak of "**backbiting**" going on in organizations as employees jostle for superior ranking in the organization.

What is enlightening to Burke is that, while various animal species seem to have a single "natural" hierarchy, humans have innumerable **"symbolic" hierarchies**. The Greek word *hieros*, translated "priest," when combined with the Greek word *archē*, meaning "first," produces the word "hierarchy." Even in the Catholic Church, there are priests who seek higher and higher positions. The highest or first priest in the Catholic Church would be higher than Bishop, Archbishop, or Cardinal: the Pope. Yet, the hierarchy goes even higher—to Jesus and God the Father. The bottom level of the hierarchy also goes lower than the lowest priest—to altar boy, parishioner, Protestant Christian, member of another religion altogether, atheist, and (eventually) Satan. This is, of course, a **religious hierarchy**. There are **educational hierarchies**—with

Ph.D.s at the top and illiterate grade school drop-outs at the bottom. There are **athletic hierarchies** as numerous as the number of events in the Winter and Summer Olympics, plus all organized (and unorganized) sports. There are **corporate hierarchies** at every corporation, as employees climb the corporate ladder. There are **popularity hierarchies** in Middle School. I comment, on pages 306-307 of my chapter, "Communication, Hierarchy, and Dramatistic Form," in Omar Swartz's book, *Transformative Communication Studies*:

> Another hierarchy is the family hierarchy. We call the competition among children in this hierarchy "sibling rivalry." Politics is a hierarchy . . . humans create all kinds of symbolic hierarchies—from the best tobacco spitter in Tennessee to the best practitioner of speaking the English language in Britain, to the best looking hand model in Hollywood. Ironically, many of those who oppose hierarchy theoretically create their own new hierarchies, such as the hierarchy of "least hierarchical systems."

Just as humans are symbol-*making*,

Inventors of the negative,

And tool-*making*,

They are also, now, hierarchy-*making*.

Bottom line . . . humans *make* things, and they *make* things using their *symbolic* nature.

Almost everything Genesis claims that God *made* was *made* by God using his *symbolic* nature— he spoke. This symbolic nature (of both man and God) is what Burke could have referred to when he said that man was goaded by a *spirit* of hierarchy. (*Spirit* is, for Burke, another word for *symbolicity*.) While other animals *have* hierarchies, their hierarchies are *not of their own making*. The other animals utilize hierarchies that already exist in nature. Humans are different. Rhetorically, one could argue that they are capable of making things due to their symbolic nature as the "image of God," the Creator.

As first mentioned in Chapter 7:

> The term "create" is used by Genesis only in terms of creating the "heavens and the Earth" in 1:1 (which seems to imply [in the term "heavens"] that the Sun, Moon, and stars were already created by Day One), creating "the great creatures of the sea and every living" thing in the sea in 1:21 (the beginning of animal life), and God creating "man in his own image" in 1:27.

Other activities of God in the creation week are described as God *making* things. *Making* could be thought of as less impressive than (but certainly in the same order as) *creating*. Furthermore (based upon the Genesis 1:2 claim that the universe that God created was originally "without form and void"), the creation week account was essentially an account of God bringing this chaos into *order*. First universe/mass, then light, then seas, then plant life, then water-based animal life, then birds, then amphibians, then land-based animal life, then mammals, and finally humans. This **bringing to order** was often essentially God *making* something out of something that he had already created. God, according to Genesis, *created* the heavens and the Earth, but *order* needed to be brought to the Earth. With the exception of animal life and human life in God's image, all of the other acts in the creation week consisted of *making*. Even the contentious issue of God's providing the Sun, Moon, and Stars as indicators of days, seasons, and years (on the 4th day) was a matter of God *making, not creating*. That is, things that he had already created (Sun, Moon, and Stars) were now *made* to serve as time markers. It was not until the heated waters above the Earth had sufficiently condensed that these preexisting (already created) celestial bodies could be made into "tools" for keeping time. Likewise, the tool-making animal (man) takes elements that already exist in his natural environment and *makes* them into useful instruments. Humans bring further *order* into the universe.

Now, what about God's hierarchy? My book *Revelation: The Human Drama* considers the hierarchical order of beings in the heavenly realm: First God (the one who is seated on the throne), then the Lamb, then the twenty-four elders (who may be a combination of the twelve apostles and the twelve sons of Israel). Beyond these, John equates all Christians--priests, prophets, saints (and even angels)—as "servants." There appears to be no hierarchy, except that of the two who in Revelation are worthy of worship (God and the Lamb). I discuss this hierarchy thoroughly on pages 145-148 of my book.

In both creation week and the heavenly hierarchy, one could say that God was "moved by a sense of order." This is precisely the language used by Burke to describe humans. Since they are also "moved by a sense of order," one could say that humans are the image of God.

This entire discussion of the definition of man (and its correlation with the definition of God) pertains to the relationship between Anthropology and religion. Disney rhetoric concerning humans does not engage issues of the origin of man, as does Anthropology. Why not? Nevertheless, WDW presents the achievements of man as something to be celebrated. WDW seems to hold humans in very high regard. This may be due to the influence of Christian Realism on Disney. Scientific Realism, in accordance with Occam's razor, ignores any supernatural characteristics of humans.

Photos of the chimney sweeps in the Mary Poppins scene in "The Great Movie Ride" in HS, the gorillas in "Pangani Forest" in the AK, and "The Hall of Presidents" in the MK.

More Photos

Chapter 15

Man's Perfectionist Tendencies=God's Image?

Assignment #16: Ride the "Tomorrowland Transit Authority" in the MK, and pay close attention to the model view of the perfect community, on your way as you approach "Space Mountain." Then, visit Disney's "perfect community"—Celebration, Florida--located directly south of the MK and Disney property, on World Drive.

Is there such a thing as a "perfect" community, a perfect chair, a perfect house, a perfect wife or husband? Kenneth Burke concluded his definition of human with what he called a "wry codicil." The fifth phrase is presented by Burke as a "final codicil [which] was still needed, thus making in all":

[The hu]Man is

the symbol-using . . . animal

inventor of the negative . . .

separated from his natural condition by instruments of his own making goaded by the spirit of hierarchy . . .

and rotten with perfection.

Phrase 5: "Rotten with Perfection." Is there such a thing as "perfect" anything? Plato thought so. In **Plato's philosophy**, there was a heavenly family of perfect forms that pre-existed all less-than-perfect forms on Earth. The very reason Plato presents his teacher Socrates asking **"Socratic" questions** is that he believed each human soul originally existed in a perfect world PRIOR to being born into human bodies. In their pre-existing state, these souls knew all perfect forms. When these souls were born, they went through a process of "forgetting" everything they originally knew. Therefore, the best way to find knowledge, for Plato and Socrates, is through a process of un-forgetting what we originally knew. Hence, Socrates asks questions. He expects his students to un-forget/remember those things they knew before birth.

Aristotle disagreed with Plato, his teacher.   He did not teach that a world of perfect forms existed in a heavenly realm; instead, his form of perfectionism related to a term he coined: **entelechy**. He taught, for example, that all living organisms have a perfect form toward which they grow.   A kernel of corn begins very small, but grows to be a stalk eight feet tall, with tassels, leaves, and ears growing within the protection of the leaves. The ears have husks, silks, cobs, and new kernels of corn growing on the cobs. The production of these new kernels represents perfection. Then, the new kernels are planted and the entelechy process starts all over again.

Kenneth Burke liked Aristotle's term entelechy, but he used it in a way different from the way Aristotle used it. Burke used the term entelechy to demonstrate that humans are always trying to chase perfection. Thus, Burke's definition of the human ends with the human's rotten obsession with *chasing perfection*. Perhaps, the *irony* of ending his definition with a clause indicating the rottenness of the human preoccupation with perfection prompted Burke to call this final phrase a "wry codicil." A *codicil* is a "small addition." It is typically used with legal documents such as wills/testaments. If an individual already has a will, but wants to make a small addition to it, such as by "adding a new piece of property and directing to whom it should go," s/he need not redo the whole will; s/he may just add a codicil. *Wry* means "dryly humorous, often with a touch of irony." Burke was hinting that there was something ironically humorous in his addition of the words "rotten with perfection" to his definition of human. I think Burke thought it both ironic and dryly humorous that *with the addition of this "perfection" codicil, Burke believes that he has "perfected" a definition of mankind.*

For my part, my doctoral dissertation at Purdue University and my book, *Implicit Rhetoric: Kenneth Burke's Extension of Aristotle's Concept of Entelechy*, detail my research into this perfectionist tendency in humans.

Walt Disney's perfectionist impulse is found in his desire to build an **Experimental Prototype Community of Tomorrow (EPCOT)**. This dream/concept of a perfect community is found in the "Tomorrowland Transit Authority" in the MK, in the model view of the perfect community, as you approach "Space Mountain." It was his original idea for EPCOT, but the later developers of EPCOT took that theme park in a different direction. Yet, Disney's "perfect community" was actually built in a newly developed town on the southern perimeter of Walt Disney World property: Celebration, Florida.

Disney's perfectionist impulse is also found in **his stories**. You will not be disappointed when you reach the end of a Walt Disney movie. He solves all of the problems raised in the movie, with a perfect solution.

Assignment #17: Walk through "Cinderella Castle" in the MK. Note the series of five scenes made of mosaic tiles on the left as you enter from Main Street. The first scene depicts a problem--Cinderella working among the cinders. Note what is happening in the three middle scenes. In the final scene, Cinderella is carried away by her prince on his white horse. Perfection!

Humans, says Burke, are rotten with perfection. We believe there is a perfect *way of speaking* a language, so we "correct" each other when our speech displays "imperfections." We believe there really is a perfect *wife*, a perfect *husband*, a perfect *child*, a perfect *church*, a perfect *mother*, and (for religionists) a perfect *father*: God.   It is with this perfect father/God in mind that Kenneth Burke introduces his term Logology.   Burke, being an *agnostic*, is not ready to embrace full-fledged Theology, but he certainly recognizes that implicit in the human discussion of Theology is the ability to conceive of and talk about perfection.   **Logology** is the *study of words*.   This study of words includes *words for the perfect, the supernatural, the theological*.   What is the term *omniscient*, as applied to God, if not a conception of someone who has *perfect knowledge*?   The term *omnipotent*, if not a conception of someone who has *perfect power*?   The term *omnipresent*, if not a conception of someone who has *perfect capacity to be present* (everywhere)?   The term *eternal*, if not a conception of someone who has perfect *longevity*?   The term *immortal*, if not a conception of someone who has perfect *living-capacity*?

How is it that, among animals, only humans show signs of conceiving of this perfection? Humans can not only conceive of a **perfectly "good" being**, but also of a **perfectly "evil" being**.   What other animal shows signs of believing in a perfect devil?   Other animals may be aware of their own predators and fear them, but do they ever perfect this notion into a concept of ultimate, perfect evil?

Assignment #18:   View "Fantasmic" in the evening at HS.   You will experience Mickey Mouse's dream of "Light vs. Darkness."   Make a list of Disney's villains portrayed in this presentation.   Do they come close to the concept of perfect evil?

Genesis 3:5 observes this nature in man—his ability to know both good and evil—and suggests that this ability makes man like God.   The serpent says to Eve: "God knows that whenever you eat of [the Tree of the Knowledge of Good and Evil], your eyes will be opened and you will, like gods, be knowing good and evil."   This Tree of the Knowledge of Good and Evil was, according to Genesis 2:9, in the center of the Garden of Eden, alongside the Tree of Life.   (Disney's AK has a Tree of Life, but no Tree of the Knowledge of Good and Evil.)   It would be in character for the serpent of Genesis to *distort the truth*, but there certainly is evidence (even in the name of the Tree) that the ability to conceive of good and evil is godlike.   The fact that man has the ability to conceive of a perfect being is one more rhetorical argument that man is in God's image.

At what point, then, could Christian Realists say that man began to exist "in God's image"? If one accepts the view of the serpent in Genesis, it may not have ultimately occurred until Adam and Eve ate from the Tree of the Knowledge of Good and Evil. (Incidentally, according to Genesis, it was not until after this event that humans made clothing from fig leaves.) If one wants to trace the origin of man to human symbol-use (as in Burke's first phrase), one would do well to look at the earliest cave drawings. If one wants to trace the fossil record to the date at which humans began to make tools (as in Burke's third phrase), it is called the Stone Age. These various different dates rely, in large part, on the calculations of Scientific Realists—Anthropologists.

It may strike the reader as strange that Burke's philosophy has no need of a definitive position on human origins. Burke answers such a question this way: "Certain . . . decisions might be immaterial to a given philosophy. For instance, though specialists might quarrel as to just exactly where human culture began and exactly how it spread, many such decisions would be quite irrelevant to a philosophy of language which takes as its starting point a definition of [hu]man as [s/]he is, everywhere all over the world, regardless of how [s/]he came to be that way" ("Poetics and Communication," in *Perspectives in Education, Religion, and the Arts*).

Individual Christian Realists may develop their own views of exactly when humans began to exist in God's image, but it seems clear that the fossil remains of pre-humans from millions of years ago that exhibited no signs of symbol-use, morality, tool-making, symbolic hierarchies, or concepts of perfection would not be in the image of the God, according to Genesis. The oldest known written languages date back some 6000 to 10,000 years. The entire matter of "not knowing" must be frustrating to a being who is "rotten with perfection"—a being who desires perfect information concerning his own origins; a being who is not God, but who views himself as having been created in the image of God. If we were not perfectionists, why would we be frustrated about this? Realists, whether of the Scientific or Christian variety, are always frustrated when there is some "truth" they do not know.

Photos the perfect community in "Tomorrowland Transit Authority," "Space Mountain," and "Cinderella Castle" in the MK, and Celebration, Florida

Chapter 16

The Afterlife

Assignment #19: Ride either the "Hollywood Tower of Terror" in HS or the "Haunted Mansion" at the MK, and pay close attention to the various depictions of ghosts. Are there such things as ghosts? What happens to humans after they die?

In addition to the concern with a definition of man, Anthropologists are interested in human views of the afterlife. Dennis O'Neil, on the website "Evolution of Modern Humans: Archaic Human Culture" (http://anthro.palomar.edu/homo2/mod_homo_3.htm), writes: "The Neandertal ritual burial of their own dead implies a belief in an afterlife. This is basically a rudimentary religious concept. Likewise, the ritual burial of cave bear trophy heads is consistent with a supernatural belief system."

Kenneth Burke, after generating his Definition of Man, toyed with the notion that he should have included one more phrase, "conscious of his own death." Not only are humans conscious of their own death, their perfectionist nature makes them interested in what happens to them after death.

Human perfectionism causes individuals to write wills and purchase life insurance to effect proper conditions *for their loved ones*, after they die. Humans also pursue methods of insuring that *their own personal afterlife* will be satisfactory.

Even **atheists**, according to Burke, are probably plagued with a haunting concern that they might find themselves in some version of Hell. Burke, an **agnostic**, sees that "atheism . . . involves the denial of immortality." His perspective will not allow him to be an atheist. He explains on pages 51-52 of *Attitudes Toward History*:

> Usually, the "scientific" mind prefers simply to truncate its thinking on the subject. It "suspends judgment." "Maybe there is immortality, and maybe there isn't." At least, if science abides by its rules, adopting a conviction only when it can be "proved by the evidence," it would not seem possible for the "scientific mind" to go beyond this agnostic position. Atheism (and, in keeping, a categorical denial of immortality) is a statement of faith that necessarily cannot be substantiated by a "weighing of all the evidence." When you find a [hu]man . . . eager to deny the possibility . . . you may legitimately . . . [ask:] Why such zest? Might it not come from a fear of punishment after death?

As for the Walt Disney Corporation, the concept of death and rebirth seems to be formulaic in Disney films. In *The Jungle Book*, Balou the Bear appears to have died, then reemerges from this state. *Sleeping Beauty* succumbs to a death-like sleep and is then awakened. Likewise, *Snow White*, after eating a poisoned apple, is laid out in a coffin by the Dwarfs until her prince revives her with a kiss. In *Pinocchio* and *Beauty and the Beast*, Pinocchio and the beast seem to actually die. Then, they are both reborn to a new kind of body: a human body, instead of a wooden puppet or beast. In a similar vein, *Hercules* descends to Hades to rescue Meg, and Mufassa, the *Lion King* Simba's father, returns from the dead to speak to Simba.

Walt Disney, according to a myth, hedged his bets. The myth says he had his body preserved by **cryogenics** at his death, so that he could be revived when the cures to his illnesses had been discovered. **Not true.** Walt died of cancer and a heart attack, on December 15, 1966. His body was cremated two days later.

Biblically, the Hebrew word *she'ol*, translated "grave, hades, or the abode of the dead," hints at the basic problem. It comes from the verb *sha'al*, meaning "to ask." A **basic rhetorical point** (frustrating to Christian Realists and Scientific Realists alike and much like the whole issue of theology) is that *there are certain things no living human knows for certain.* We may, at times, just need to leave some things in the arena of things we are still "asking" about. Therefore, the afterlife and theology, in general, fall in the realm of *rhetoric.* There seems to be evidence, dating as far back as the Neanderthals, that humans have believed in an afterlife. As Burke suggests, it would appear to be beyond the capacity of science to either prove or disprove the existence of either the afterlife or God. So, where are we?

Humans have been persuading themselves and others for thousands of years regarding such religious issues as are found lurking in the parks at WDW. Some would persuade others that, since we do not know the answers of *she'ol*, we need not even consider it. Others would persuade that, since there is an *instinctive* view in humans that there is an afterlife, we would be unwise to ignore such issues. Some would persuade that, if there is an afterlife, everyone will (in a Disneyesque sense) "live happily ever after." Other would persuade that, if there is an afterlife, some will live happier ever after than others. The question rhetoric poses is: Since we do not know for certain, what do you think?

Photos of "Hollywood Tower of Terror" in HS and the "Haunted Mansion" at the MK

More Photos

Chapter 17

Conclusion

Your research has taken you through the four theme parks of WDW in search of religious rhetoric. While some view rhetoric as the *act* of persuading, Aristotle (who, more than two thousand years ago), wrote the seminal book on the subject, *On Rhetoric*, called it *the faculty of seeing in each situation the available means of persuasion*. It is not designed to prove things absolutely. Such would be the goal of *dialectic*, in Aristotle's system—the discovery of *absolute truth*. This does not mean that rhetoric is not concerned with the truth. If that were the case, Christian Realists and Scientific Realists would not be interested in rhetoric, at all. Instead, rhetoric aims at the discovery of *probable truth*. Rhetoric never *totally* proves anything. It operates only in the realm of those matters of truth that *cannot be known absolutely*. Rhetoric discovers the *means* by which persuasion concerning probable truth may be accomplished.

This book has tackled the rhetorical task of seeing the available means of *transcending the divisions between Christian Realists and Scientific Realists*. That task was prompted by indications that somehow Walt Disney and the creators of WDW were comfortable with rhetoric supplied by both Christian Realist and Scientific Realist perspectives (often thought of as opposite perspectives). Both perspectives are presented in WDW.

In locating *means* of persuading Christian Realists of the views of Scientific Realists, this book takes into account the fact that Christian Realists believe truth is to be found in the Bible. Any attempts to find persuasive materials should look to the writings contained therein and not discount them. Hence, the persuasive arguments presented to Christian Realists typically demonstrated possible alternative interpretations of Scripture. These interpretations were shown to be in general harmony with the views of Scientific Realists, with the primary exception that God, as agent, was inserted into the perspective.

In locating *means* of persuading Scientific Realists of the views of Christian Realists, this book takes into account the fact that Scientific Realists believe truth is to be found in fossil records, physics, geology, biology, and anthropology. Any attempts to find persuasive materials should look to the findings of science, and not discount them. Hence, the persuasive arguments presented to Scientific Realists typically demonstrated that possible alternative interpretations of Scripture were in general harmony with the views of Scientific Realists, with the primary exception that God, as agent, was inserted into the perspective. Furthermore, since a major stumbling block for Scientific Realists in accepting the views of Christian Realists is their commitment to employing Occam's razor, persuasive arguments were presented to call Occam's razor into doubt. In its place, Aristotelian and Burkean perspectives on Dramatism were suggested.

WDW certainly may have motives other than a need to reconcile competing Realist perspectives that would account for the combination of the perspectives of Scientific Realists and Christian Realists. There is the **financial motive**: WDW does not want to offend any potential patrons, so it includes both views. There is the **social motive**: WDW may be avoiding overt references to evolution (just as it presents both political parties in its "Hall of Presidents" and "American Adventure") to appear to be fair-minded. If it were not that Walt, himself, made comments indicative of a belief in God and a belief in science, it might be just as useful to avoid any discussion of religious rhetoric at WDW. Yet, when one discovers such evidence as Lincoln's belief in "divine providence," quoting Jesus from Mark 3:25, asserting that all men are "created" equal and stating "I know there is a God," and Walt remarking, "I know drinking and smoking are sins because you aren't taking care of the body God gave you," one cannot help but believe there is a **religious motive** at work, as well.

When one sees in the "Universe of Energy" attraction a wholly god-less perspective, considers the 1950s *Disneyland* television series that presented the history of evolution as it is shown in the "Rite of Spring" sequence from *Fantasia*, visits the Cretaceous Era which WDW estimates occurred 65 million years ago, and sees depictions of humans developing culture, beginning with caveman, one senses that a **central rhetorical conflict** is present. It just seems logical to explore the religious rhetoric at WDW.

Bibliography

Works by Kenneth Burke

Burke, Kenneth. *Attitudes Toward History*. 3rd ed. Berkeley: Univ. of California Press, 1984.

---. *Attitudes Toward History*. 2 vols. New York: New Republic, 1937.

---. *The Complete White Oxen*. Berkeley: Univ. of California Press, 1968.

---. "Counter-Gridlock: An Interview with Kenneth Burke*" All Area*, vol 2 (Spring, 1983): 4-31.

---. *Counter-Statement*. Berkeley: Univ. of California Press, 1968.

---. "Dramatism." In *Communication: Concepts and Perspectives*. Edited by Lee Thayer. 327-360. Washington, DC: Spartan Books, 1967.

---. *Dramatism and Development*. Barre, MA: Clark Univ. Press with Barre Publishers, 1972.

---. "The Five Master Terms: Their Place in a 'Dramatistic' Grammar of Motives." *View* 3, no. 2 (1943): 50-52.

---. "Freedom and Authority in the Realm of the Poetic Imagination." In *Freedom and Authority in Our Time*. Edited by Lyman Bryson, Louis Finkelstein, R. M. MacIver, and Richard McKeon. 365-375. New York and London: Harper & Brothers, 1953.

---. *A Grammar of Motives*. Berkeley: Univ. of California Press, 1969.

---. *Language as Symbolic Action: Essays on Life, Literature, and Method*. Berkeley: Univ. of California Press, 1966.

---. "On Catharsis or Resolution, with a Postscript." *Kenyon Review* 21 (1959): 337-375.

---. "On Human Behavior Considered 'Dramatistically.'" In *Permanence and Change: An Anatomy of Purpose*. 2nd ed. 274-294. Indianapolis: Bobbs-Merrill, 1975.

---. "On Stress, Its Seeking" in *Why Man Takes Chances: Studies in Stress-Seeking*. Edited by Samuel Z. Klausner. 75-103. Garden City, NY: Doubleday, 1968.

---. *On Symbols and Society*. Edited by Joseph R. Gusfield. Chicago and London: Univ. of Chicago Press, 1989.

---. "Othello—An Essay to Illustrate a Method." In *Perspectives by Incongruity*. Edited by Stanley Edgar Hyman. 152-195. Bloomington: Indiana Univ. Press, 1964.

---. *Permanence and Change: An Anatomy of Purpose*. 2nd ed. Indianapolis: The Bobbs-Merrill Company, Inc., 1975.

---. *The Philosophy of Literary Form: Studies in Symbolic Action*. 3rd ed. Berkeley: Univ. of California Press, 1973.

---. "Poetics and Communication." In *Perspectives in Education, Religion, and the Arts*. Edited by Howard E Kiefer and Milton K. Munitz. 401-418. Albany: State Univ. of New York Press, 1970.

---. "Questions and Answers about the Pentad." *College Composition and Communication* 29 (1978): 330-335.

---. "The Rhetorical Situation." In *Communication: Ethical and Moral Issues*. Edited by Lee Thayer. 263-275. London, New York, Paris: Gordon and Breach Science Publishers, 1973.

---. *A Rhetoric of Motives*. Berkeley: Univ. of California Press, 1969.

---. *The Rhetoric of Religion*. Boston: Beacon Press, 1961.

---. "Rhetoric—Old and New." In *New Rhetorics*. Edited by Martin Steinmann, Jr. 59-76. New York: Scribner's Sons, 1967.

---. "Rhetoric, Poetics, and Philosophy." In *Rhetoric, Philosophy, and Literature*. Edited by Don M. Burks. 15-33. West Lafayette, IN: Purdue Univ. Press, 1978.

---. *The Selected Correspondence of Kenneth Burke and Malcolm Cowley 1915-1981*. Edited by Paul Jay. Berkeley: Univ. of California Press, 1990.

---. "Tactics of Motivation*" Chimera*, vol 1 (1943): 27-44.

---. "Theology and Logology (Abstract)." *Journal of the American Academy of Religion* 47 (1979): 298.

---. "Theology & Logology*" Kenyon Review*, New Series, vol I # 1, Winter 1979.

---. *Towards a Better Life*. Berkeley: Univ. of California Press, 1982.

Works about Kenneth Burke

Burks, Don M. "Dramatic Irony, Collaboration, and Kenneth Burke's Theory of Form." *Pre/Text* 6 (1985): 255-273.

---. *Rhetoric, Philosophy, and Literature: An Exploration*. West Lafayette, IN: Purdue Univ. Press, 1978.

Cowley, Malcolm. "Prolegomena to Kenneth Burke." In *Critical Responses to Kenneth Burke*. Edited by William R. Rueckert. 247-251. Minneapolis: Univ. of Minnesota Press, 1969.

Donoghue, Denis. "American Sage." *The New York Review* 26 (September, 1985): 39-42.

Foss, Sonja K., Karen A. Foss, and Robert Trapp. *Contemporary Perspectives on Rhetoric.* 2nd ed. Prospect Heights, IL: Waveland Press, 1991.

Griffin, Leland M. "A Dramatistic Theory of the Rhetoric of Movements." In *Critical Responses to Kenneth Burke*. Edited by William R. Rueckert. 456-478. Minneapolis: Univ. of Minnesota Press, 1969.

Hart, Roderick P. *Modern Rhetorical Criticism.* Glenview, IL and London: Scott, Foresman/Little, Brown, 1990.

Howell, Wilbur Samuel. *Poetics, Rhetoric, and Logic.* Ithaca and London: Cornell Univ. Press, 1975.

Jennermann, Donald L. "Kenneth Burke's Poetics of Catharsis." In *Representing Kenneth Burke*. Edited by Hayden White and Margaret Brose. 31-51. Baltimore and London: John Hopkins Univ. Press, 1982.

---. "The Literary Criticism and Theory of Kenneth Burke in Light of Aristotle, Freud, and Marx." Ph.D. diss., Indiana Univ., 1974.

Lindsay, Stan A. *Basic Public Relations Documents.* Orlando: Say Press, 2010.

---. "The Burkean Entelechy and the Apocalypse of John." Ph.D. diss., Purdue Univ., 1995.

---. "Communication, Hierarchy, and Dramatistic Form: The Arousing and Relieving of Stress." In *Transformative Communication Studies: Culture, Hierarchy and the Human Condition*. Edited by Omar Swartz. Leicester, UK: Troubador Publishing Ltd., 2008.

---. *A Concise Kenneth Burke Concordance.* W. Lafayette, IN: Say Press, 2004.

---. *The Essence of Rhetoric in Disney Music.* Orlando: Say Press, 2010.

---. *Implicit Rhetoric: Kenneth Burke's Extension of Aristotle's Concept of Entelechy.* Lanham, MD: Univ. Press of America, 1998.

---. *Persuasion, Proposals, and Public Speaking.* 2nd ed. Orlando: Say Press, 2009.

---. *Psychotic Entelechy: The Dangers of "Spiritual Gift" Theology.* Lanham, MD: Univ. Press of America, 2005.

---. *Revelation: The Human Drama.* Bethlehem, PA: Lehigh Univ. Press, 2001.

---. *The Seven Cs of Stress: A Burkean Approach.* W. Lafayette, IN: Say Press, 2004.

---. *The Twenty-One Sales in a Sale.* Grants Pass, OR: Oasis Books/PSI Research, 1998.

---. "Waco and Andover: An Application of Kenneth Burke's Concept of Psychotic Entelechy" *Quarterly Journal of Speech*, vol 85 (1999): 268-284.

Nichols, Marie Hochmuth. "Burkeian Criticism." In *Essays on Rhetorical Criticism.* Edited by Thomas R. Nilsen. New York: Random House, 1968.

---. "Kenneth Burke and the 'New Rhetoric.'" In *Contemporary Theories of Rhetoric: Selected Readings.* Edited by Richard L. Johannesen. New York, Evanston, San Francisco, London: Harper and Row, 1971.

Rucckert, William H. *Critical Responses to Kenneth Burke.* Minneapolis: Univ. of Minnesota Press, 1969.

---. *Encounters with Kenneth Burke.* Urbana and Chicago: Univ. of Illinois Press, 1994.

---. *Kenneth Burke and the Drama of Human Relations.* 2nd ed. Berkeley: Univ. of California Press, 1963).

---. "The Rhetoric of Rebirth: A Study of the Literary Theory and Critical Practice of Kenneth Burke." Ph.D. diss., Univ. of Michigan, 1956.

Schiappa, Edward. "Burkean Tropes and Kuhnian Science: A Social Constructionist Perspective on Language and Reality." *Journal of Advanced Communication* 13 (1993): 401-422.

White, Hayden, and Margaret Brose, Editors. *Representing Kenneth Burke.* Baltimore and London: John Hopkins Univ. Press, 1982.

Winterowd, W. Ross. "Kenneth Burke: An annotated Glossary of His Terministic Screen and a 'Statistical' Survey of His Major Concepts." *Rhetoric Society Quarterly* 15 (1985): 145-177.

Works by and about Aristotle

Aristotle. *De Anima.* Translated by J. A. Smith. Oxford: At the Clarendon Press, 1931. Reprinted in *The Works of Aristotle Translated into English.* Edited by W. D. Ross. Oxford: Clarendon Press, 1968.

---. *On Sophistical Refutations, On Coming-to-Be and Passing Away.* Translated by E. S. Forster. Cambridge: Harvard Univ. Press, 1955.

---. *Physica.* Translated by R. P. Hardie and R. K. Gaye. In *The Basic Works of Aristotle.* Edited by Richard McKeon. New York: Random House, 1941.

---. *Poetics.* Translated by T. S. Dorsch. In *Classical Literary Criticism.* London: Penguin Books, 1965.

---. *The Rhetoric and the Poetics of Aristotle.* Edited by Friedrich Solmsen. New York: Random House, 1954.

Kennedy, George A. *Aristotle On Rhetoric.* New York and Oxford: Oxford Univ. Press, 1991.

McKeon, Richard. *The Basic Works of Aristotle.* New York: Random House, 1941.

---. *Introduction to Aristotle.* 2nd ed. Chicago and London: Univ. of Chicago Press, 1973.

Randall, John Herman, Jr. *Aristotle.* New York: Columbia Univ. Press, 1960.

Ross, W.D. *Aristotle (A Complete Exposition of his Works & Thought).* New York: Meridian Books, 1960.

---. *Aristotle De Anima.* Oxford: Clarendon Press, 1961.

---. *Aristotle's Metaphysics.* 2 vols. Oxford: Clarendon Press, 1966.

---. *Aristotle's Physics.* Oxford: Clarendon Press, 1966.

---. *Metaphysica.* vol. 8 of *The Works of Aristotle Translated into English.* Oxford: Clarendon Press, 1966.

Williams, C. J. F. *Aristotle's De Generatione et Corruptione.* Oxford: Clarendon Press, 1982.

Works about Walt Disney

Anderson, Philip L. *The Gospel in Disney: Christian Values in the Early Animated Classics.* Minneapolis, MN: Augsburg Fortress Publishers, 1993.

Bell, Elizabeth, Lynda Haas, and Laura Sells, Editors. *From Mouse to Mermaid: The Politics of Film, Gender, and Culture.* Bloomington, IN: Indiana Univ. Press, 1995.

Byrne, Eleanor, and Martin McQuillan. *Deconstructing Disney.* Pluto Press, 2000.

Giroux, Henry A. *The Mouse that Roared: Disney and the End of Innocence.* Lanham, MD: Rowman & Littlefield Publishers, 2001.

Pinsky, Mark I. *The Gospel According to Disney: Faith, Trust, and Pixie Dust.* Louisville, KY: Westminster John Knox Press, 2004.

Watts, Steven. *The Magic Kingdom: Walt Disney and the American Way of Life.* Columbia, MO: Univ. of Missouri Press, 2001.

Various Works

Allen, James. *The First Year of Greek*. rev. ed. Toronto: MacMillan, 1931.

Best, Stephen, and Douglas Kellner. *Postmodern Theory: Critical Interrogations*. New York: The Guilford Press.

Cassirer, Ernst. *Language and Myth*. Translated by Susanne K. Langer. New York: Dover Publications, Inc., 1946.

"Egyptian Hieroglyphics." In *Virtual-Egypt.com*. Web. 28 March 2010.

Einstein, Albert. "Einstein Explains the Equivalence of Energy and Matter." Web. 28 March 2010.

Fischel, Henry A. *Rabbinic Literature and Greco-Roman Philosophy*. Leiden: E. J. Brill, 1973.

Fishman, Isidore. *Gateway to the Mishnah*. Hartmore, CT: Prayer Book Press, Inc., 1970.

Frisk, Hjalmar. *Griechisches Etymologisches Woerterbuch*. 2 vols. Heidelberg: Carl Winter Universitatsverlag, 1960.

"God." In *The New World Encyclopedia*. Web. 28 March 2010.

Homer. *The Iliad of Homer*. Translated by Richmond Lattimore. Chicago and London: Univ. of Chicago Press, 1961.

Keating, Gina. "Christian Filmmakers Praise Walt, Fault Disney Co." In Reuters. Web. 28 March 2010.

Kirby, John T. "Classics 593R: Classical Concepts of Rhetoric and Poetics," lecture delivered in graduate seminar at Purdue Univ., West Lafayette, IN, 3 February 1994.

---. "The 'Great Triangle' in Early Greek Rhetoric and Poetics." *Rhetorica* 8 (1990): 213-228.

---. "Rhetorical Theory in Bronze-Age Greece?" lecture delivered at the Purdue Univ. Colloquium for Center for Humanistic Studies, West Lafayette, IN, 18 April 1994.

Liddell, Henry George, and Robert Scott. Compilers. *A Greek-English Lexicon.* Revised by Henry Stuart Jones. Oxford: Clarendon Press, 1968.

---. *A Lexicon Abridged from Liddell and Scott's Greek-English Lexicon.* Oxford: Clarendon Press, 1966.

Lightfoot, J. B. *The Apostolic Fathers.* Edited by J. R. Harmer. Grand Rapids, MI: Baker Book House, 1956.

"Missing Link." In *All about Science.* Web. 28 March 2010.

Mitchell, Esther. "Hercules, Greek Hero, God, Myth." Web. 28 March 2010.

Plato. *Plato: Phaedrus and The Seventh and Eighth Letters.* Translated by Walter Hamilton. New York: Penguin Books, 1973.

Schiappa, Edward. "History and Neo-Sophistic Criticism: A Reply to Poulakos." *Philosophy and Rhetoric* 23 (1990), 307-315.

---. Editor. *Landmark Essays on Classical Greek Rhetoric.* Davis, CA: Hermagoras Press, 1994.

---. "Neo-Sophistic Rhetorical Criticism or the Historical Reconstruction of Sophistic Doctrines?" *Philosophy and Rhetoric* 23 (1990), 192-217.

---. "*Rhetorikê*: What's in a Name? Toward a Revised History of Early Greek Rhetorical Theory." *Quarterly Journal of Speech* 78 (1992): 1-15.

Index

Worksheet for Studying this Book

Your Name:_____

1. Fill in the following quotes from/about President Abraham Lincoln in the "Hall of Presidents":

    a. Douglas mentions Lincoln's belief in "_____ providence" in their debates.

    b. "A _____ divided against itself cannot stand."

    c. "All men are _____ equal."

    d. "I know there is a _____ and that he hates injustice and slavery. I see a storm coming; I know his _____ is in it."

2. What "Shoppe" in the MK, celebrates the Christmas holiday?
   _____

3. Indiana Jones in HS searches for the lost Ark of the _____.

4. Walt Disney once remarked, "I know drinking and smoking are _____ because you aren't taking care of the body _____ gave you."

5.   In the 1950s, the _____ television series on ABC TV aired an episode that presented the history of evolution in a fashion similar to that in which it is shown in the "Rite of Spring" sequence from *Fantasia*.

6.   Small children are able to "research" the fossil record at the "_____" playground and along the "Cretaceous Trail" at AK.

7.   In the attraction "Dinosaur" at the AK, you will time travel backwards to the Cretaceous Era, which the Disney ride estimates, occurred _____ years ago.

8.   "Spaceship Earth" in EPCOT present human culture, beginning with _____.

9.   _____ was a Realist who believed that truth existed in a non-earthly realm of the ideal. _____ questioning helps humans *unforget* the truth.

10.   Plato's student _____ saw truth in the *sensory* world rather than in some other-worldly realm.

11.   The seventeenth century philosopher Rene _____ was a Realist who is credited with founding Modernism.

12.   _____ doubt is the basis of the scientific method.

13.   Scientists make propositions that they are not entirely certain of. These uncertain propositions are called "_____."

14.   _____, following DesCartes suggested that one could doubt everything that is not *empirically verifiable* (capable of being verified by sense-data— seeing, hearing, smelling, tasting, and feeling).

15.   When _____ demonstrated that even mathematics could be doubted, Modernism effectively crumbled.

16.   In place of Modernism, _____ arose.

17.   In his essay, "The Rhetorical Situation," Burke is happy with a truth formula such as "there is _____ truth."

18.   Christian Realism believes that there is truth and that such truth has been communicated to humans by God in _____.

19.   Transcendence is a sort of *bridge between* _____.

20.   Whenever a group of people, such as scientists, identify with one another, there is "_____." This means there is a sense of *unity* felt by all members of the group.

21.   According to *The New World Encyclopedia*, "Throughout history, the vast majority of people in the world have believed in _____.

22.   _____ comes from the Greek words *anthropos* (meaning man/human) and *morphē* (meaning form/shape).

23.   _____ means that, while humans change constantly, God is unchangeable.

24.   _____ means that, while humans can only be in one place at a time, God is not confined to any single location at any specific time.

25.   _____ means that, while humans are time-bound (they are born, they live a while, and they die), God has no beginning and no end.

26.   _____ means that, while humans have been able to harness the energy of the Earth to send spacecraft to the Moon, Mars, and beyond, this power is infinitesimal compared to a God who created the entire universe (of which man's space exploration has only scratched the surface).

27.   _____ means that, while humans know many things, God knows all things.

28.   The humans, throughout history, whom society has termed "_____," have been those who seemed to know more things that most other humans.

29.   The movie *Pinocchio* featured a conscience for Pinocchio, named Jiminy Cricket (a euphemism for _____).

30.   _____ is the number #1 tourist destination in the world.

31.   Walt Disney declared _____ on October 4, 1923.

32.   In Burke's Pentad, _____ must be performed within _____ by _____ who use certain tools or _____ to perform them. What is not included of these in the game of Clue is the _____.

33.   _____ was the *agency* used most by Walt.

34.   Walt cites as his motive for creating Disneyland his experience with _____.

35.   _____ refers to *a philosophy of the origins of the universe in which an agent (God) is actively involved in the formation of everything in the universe.*

36.   Those who believe that the entire process of generating the universe began approximately 6000 years ago, beginning with the six days of creation are called _____ Earth advocates.

37.   The syllogism is the basis of _____ reasoning.

38.   _____ extends the syllogism by providing for situations in which some of the premises or conclusions might not be true.

39.   A rebuttal in Toulminian analysis *typically begins with the word* _____.

40.   In addition to the twenty-four hour denotation, the word *yom* also, at times, means

       _____

       _____.

41.   A _____ rebuts the rebuttal, in a sense. It typically begins with the word "*but.*"

42.   The **Warrant** of Toulmin is quite similar to the _____ of the syllogism.

43.   The **Data** of Toulmin represent a specific statement, nearly equivalent to the _____ of the syllogism.

44.   For Toulmin, the **Claim** is similar to the _____ of the syllogism.

45.   A _____ is an attack on either the *warrant* or the *data* or the *claim* or the *backing.*

46.   The Toulminian _____ is an adverb (such as *possibly*, *probably*, or *definitely*) that indicates the strength of the claim.

47.   The Hebrew "_____" form means that the term "beginning" in Genesis should be connected with another noun by the word "of."

48.   Aristotle's term for **Purpose** was one of Aristotle's four major _____ of action.

49. _____ is known as the **Final Cause**—the purpose for which things in nature occur.

50. _____ is known as the **Efficient Cause**.

51. _____ is known as the **Material Cause**.

52. Theologians since the second century a.d. have debated whether the universe was created *ex* _____ (out of nothing), *ex* _____ (out of some preexisting material), or *ex* _____ (out of God's nature itself).

53. According to Einstein's _____, **Mass** can be changed into **Energy**, and vice versa.

54. The _____ theory of the origins of the universe is based on the notion that "in the beginning" there was a huge conversion of Energy into Mass.

55. Disney's "Wishes" _____ presentation hints to children who may have serious or even fatal diseases that there "truly" is a force in the universe capable of performing miracles, if they truly believe.

56. "Occam's Razor," named for its inventor, _____, is the "keystone of scientific terminologies."

57. In accordance with Occam's razor, God is missing from the story of the origins of the universe in the "Universe of Energy," but, we cannot say that God is MIA (missing in "action"), because _____.

58. What would change, if God were inserted into the "Universe of Energy" exhibit?

_____

_____

59. _____ seems to be the major issue non-believers cite regarding the order of creation in the first chapter of Genesis.

60. Creation accounts have been a part of the religious traditions of the ancient cultures represented in "Spaceship Earth" and virtually all other cultures since _____ _____.

61.   The _____ focused on the role of the *Nile River* in creation. They saw the beginning as a mass of *chaotic waters*, called *Nu* or *Nun*. To this beginning they added *Sun, Moon, Earth, and Sky gods* who gave birth to *Isis* and *Osiris*.

62.   According to an account of _____ creation mythology dating at least as far back as the first century a.d., there was first *chaos*; then from a *cosmic egg*, creation of the universe began.

63.   _____ creation stories begin with *sky and sea*, and then the creation god *Kukulkan* speaks the word "Earth," and the *Earth* rises from the sea.

64.   Vying with Genesis as the oldest creation account is the _____ creation myth developed from _____ myths, in the 12th century b.c. According to this account, *god/s did not exist at the beginning* of the universe. Instead, *sweet and bitter waters comingled* and created many gods. Then, one god born of two others, *Marduk*, eventually defeated and killed the bitter waters, *Tiamat*, in a colossal struggle. *Earth* was created, followed by the *moon*, then the *Sun*. Finally, *humans* descended from the gods.

65.   _____ creation mythology began with *chaos*, a watery state ruled by *Oceanus*.

66.   *Poseidon*, one of the great Greek gods, is known by the **Romans** as _____.

67.   The most stressful and emotionally divisive debate between Scientific Realists and Christian Realists is over the issue of _____.

68.   The "logic" of evolutionists who believe that there must be more intelligent life on other planets is expressed in the **Drake Equation**, developed by _____, in 1961: $N = R_* \, f_p \, n_e \, f_l \, f_i \, f_c \, L$.

69.   A famous popularizer of astrobiology, extraterrestrial intelligent life theory, and astronomy, _____, came up with a plan for attaching some sort of message to U.S. spacecraft that may be destined to leave the Earth permanently. Some of his notions are dramatized in the 1997 movie, *Contact*.

70. On December 4, 1957, the _____ television series on ABC TV aired an episode (on the history of evolution on Earth) entitled "Mars and Beyond," directed by Ward Kimball.

71. Stephen J. Gould, America's most famous evolutionist . . . stated, "The extreme rarity of transitional forms in the _____ record persists as the trade secret of paleontology.

72. Genesis 1:11 indicates "how" God made plants. He _____ to the land.

73. The term "create" is used by Genesis only in terms of creating the _____ in 1:1 . . . creating _____ in 1:21, and God creating _____ in 1:27.

74. The second element of that catch phrase "In essentials, unity. In opinions, liberty. In all things, love." is a principle of _____ _____.

75. Kenneth Burke, in *The Rhetoric of Religion*, discusses what he calls: "_____," the defining of God in terms of what he is not.

76. A negative term Judaism adds to the description of God is "_____." The Ark of the Covenant (as presented visually in the movie Raiders of the Lost Ark) was designed to symbolically make this point.

77. **Gaia** is encountered when you are greeted by some cast members in the AK. You may also see a sign when approaching the Tree of Life that says "Viva Gaia!" Viva Gaia means "_____!" There is no statue of this ancient Greek goddess because you are standing on her. Gaia is *the Earth goddess*.

78. _____, the *Greek Horse god*, is encountered in the Great Movie Ride (in the film clip from *Fantasia*) at HS. He is the horse with wings.

79. **Kukulkan**, the *Mayan creation god*, may be seen at the _____ Pavilion in EPCOT.

80. The *Roman god of the sea*, **Neptune** (also known as the *Greek god* **Poseidon**), may be seen in the _____ pavilion at EPCOT.

81. If you are familiar with the Disney film, *The Little Mermaid*, you will know that the little mermaid's father is _____, the *sea messenger god, the son of Poseidon*.

82. One way Jews depicted the invisible God was with the Ark of the Covenant. The Ark was a chest that was believed to originally contain the two stone tablets with the engraving of the _____.

83. On the top of the Ark were images of two _____ whose wings met above the middle of the Ark.

84. Kenneth Burke claims that humans have two characteristics. Our _____ would be the *physical characteristics of humans* (similar to other animals). Our _____ would be that *invisible characteristic that makes us different from all other animals*.

85. Humans communicate by using what Burke calls "_____," while all other animals communicate by what Burke calls "_____."

86. The centerpiece in all of Walt Disney World for the study of human communication is "_____."

87. The **first attribute** of a symbol is that a **symbol** is something that _____ *something else*.

88. The **Phoenicians** developed an _____, which most western civilizations use to this day.

89. _____ provides symbols for those who may not even be able to hear words.

90. _____ provides symbols for those who cannot see.

91. A _____ is "programmed communication." The animal **instinctively** knows the meaning of the communication of its own species.

92. The **second attribute** of a symbol is that it may be _____ *chosen*.

93. The **third attribute** of a symbol is that *there must be* _____ *meaning*.

94. Man is the symbol-using (symbol-_____, symbol-misusing) . . . animal, inventor of (and _____ by) the negative . . . separated from his _____ condition by instruments of his own making, goaded by the spirit of _____ (or moved by a sense of order) . . . and rotten with _____.

95.   Burke calls the **first type of word**--words God uses in creating the world

_____.

96.   The **second type of word** God uses is _____, which has much less

power to affect humans.

97.   Burke identifies the *basis upon which he distinguishes between the two types of words*--

the _____.

98.   Clearly implied in any "Thou shalt not" is the element of _____ or

choice.

99.   We do *not* tell anyone "Thou shalt not" do something it is _____ to not

do.

100.   Jewish theology suggests that humans have both a _____ **inclination** and an

_____ **inclination.**

101.   In the sense of being "separated from his natural condition by instruments of his own

making," one could also say that *man is "super"*-_____.

102.   *Sea otters* can "use" tools (that they do not make). They can "find" _____

and use them as tools to break open the shells of shellfish, so they can eat the meat inside.

103.   *Apes* will use _____ they "find" to place in holes and crevices to retrieve

insects and other foods.

104.   Humans "make" rocks into cutting instruments. They chip away edges of the rocks to

make sharp _____—even in the *Stone Age*.

105.   Humans use vines to tie their sharp rocks to sticks and they "made" _____.

106.   Every single human culture, it seems, has learned to "make" bows and

_____.

107.   Virtually all animals have hierarchies, but (other than humans) these hierarchies are all

"_____" hierarchies.

108.   In the insect world, the top of the hierarchy is typically a _____, such as

the leader of the Bees.

109.   Among such birds as chickens, there is a "_____ order."

110.   Among wolves, the "leader of the pack" is allowed to bite the _____ of every other member of the wolf-pack.

111.   What is enlightening to Burke is that, while various animal species seem to have a single hierarchy, humans have innumerable "_____" hierarchies.

112.   The Greek word *hieros*, translated "_____," when combined with the Greek word *archē*, meaning "_____," produces the word "hierarchy."

113.   In the Catholic Church, there are priests, Bishops, Archbishops, Cardinals, and the Pope. This is a _____ hierarchy.

114.   There are _____ hierarchies—with Ph.D.s at the top and illiterate grade school drop-outs at the bottom.

115.   In the _____ hierarchy, we call the competition among children "sibling rivalry."

116.   In _____ philosophy, there was a heavenly family of perfect forms that pre-existed all less-than-perfect forms on Earth.

117.   _____ disagreed with Plato, his teacher. He did not teach that a world of perfect forms existed in a heavenly realm; instead, his form of perfectionism related to a term he coined: **entelechy**.

118.   A _____ is a "small addition." It is typically used with legal documents such as wills.

119.   _____ means "dryly humorous, often with a touch of irony." Burke was hinting that there was something ironically humorous in his addition of the words "rotten with perfection" to his definition of human. I think Burke thought it both ironic and dryly humorous that *with the addition of this "perfection" codicil, Burke believes that he has "perfected" a definition of mankind.*

120.   Walt Disney's perfectionist impulse is found in his desire to build EPCOT an **Experimental** _____ **Community of** _____.

121.   _____ is the *study of words*. This study of words includes *words for the perfect, the supernatural, the theological.*

122.   The Tree of _____ was, according to Genesis 2:9, in the center of the Garden of Eden, alongside the Tree of Life. (Disney's AK has a Tree of Life, but not this Tree.)

123.   In addition to the concern with a definition of man, _____ are interested in human views of the afterlife.

124.   The Neanderthal ritual burial of their own dead implies a belief in an afterlife. This is basically a rudimentary _____ concept.

125.   Burke, an _____, sees that "atheism . . . involves the denial of immortality."

126.   In *The Jungle Book*, _____ appears to have died, then reemerges from this state. _____, after eating a poisoned apple, is laid out in a coffin by the Dwarfs until her prince revives her with a kiss. In *Pinocchio* and *Beauty and the Beast*, Pinocchio and the beast seem to actually die. Then, they are both reborn to a new kind of body: a _____ body, instead of a wooden puppet or beast.

127.   Was Walt Disney's body preserved by **cryogenics** at his death, so that he could be revived when the cures to his illnesses had been discovered? _____

128.   Biblically, the Hebrew word *she'ol*, translated "grave, hades, or the abode of the dead," comes from the verb *sha'al*, meaning _____.

129.   *There are certain things no living human knows for certain.* Therefore, the afterlife and theology, in general, fall in the realm of _____.

130.   _____ is not designed to prove things absolutely. Such would be the goal of *dialectic*, in Aristotle's system—the discovery of *absolute truth*. Instead, it aims at the discovery of *probable truth*. It operates only in the realm of those matters of truth that *cannot be known absolutely*. It discovers the *means* by which persuasion concerning probable truth may be accomplished.

Guide for Conducting Park-by-Park Research

Your Name:_____

1. Throughout your visit to WDW, you will encounter the highest creation/being, gathered together from all over the world (and all different cultures): human beings.

2. List any evidence of the following religions at WDW:

   a. **Christianity**

   b. **Atheism**

   c. **Judaism**

   d. **Islam**

   e. **Other modern religions**

   f. **Religions of the past**

3. With or without writing them down, think about your views of the following religious issues encountered at WDW:

- What existed before the universe was formed?

- How did the universe come into being?

- Is there a god?

- What was the chronological sequence in the development of the universe, our solar system, and our planet?

- How long did it take for the world to develop to the stage it has?

- How did life originate?

- What was the chronological sequence in the development of life?

- Did life evolve from species to species? From genus to genus?

- What was the origin of humans?

- Do humans enjoy a special relationship with a divine being?

- Is there life on other planets?

- Is there an afterlife?

EPCOT:

1. Ride through "Spaceship Earth" and notice Disney's rapid presentation of the development of human communication. Beginning with _____ (which scholars date no earlier than some 30,000 years ago) humans have found ways to communicate symbolically with one another. _____ turned these simple art symbols into a language of hieroglyphics. _____

developed a more universal alphabet. _____ philosophized, and
_____ spread communication through a network of roads.

a. You are looking for symbol-use. What symbols are used in the cave drawings, hieroglyphics, sculpture, chapel artwork, movies, television, etc.?

_____

_____

b. Think about the history of human communication. List some of the developments.

_____

_____

c. List as many as you can of the tools for saving and sending (via the media) the pieces of symbolic communication the humans had "made": _____

_____

_____

2. Visit the attraction "Universe of Energy." Starting with the "Big Bang," in a very short span of time, you will view a sequence of events that many scientists believe occurred over a period of 13 to 14 billion years. What you are viewing is Disney's visual interpretation of the origins of the universe, according to accepted views in physics. List as many of the events as you can in chronological order:

_____

_____

_____

_____

a. Did you see any reference to God, there? Why do you think that is true? What would change, if God were inserted into the sequence?

_____

_____

_____

b. Pay very close attention to what Bill Nye, the science guy, calls the "big bang" and Ellen calls the "ding dang." If a sculptor plans to sculpt a statue, s/he must decide whether to sculpt it out of soap, ice, rock, gold, bronze, wood, etc. What "material" was used to form the universe, according to the film? Hint: it may be related to the name of the attraction. _____

_____

c. Notice the humorous slice-of-life demonstrating that humans learned to control fire and found that the use of that basic form of energy led to other tools for using energy. List as many as you can. _____

_____

_____

_____

3. Since you have considered the tool-making nature of human beings, explore the celebration of some of those inventions. Ride "Mission Space," to feel what it is like to space travel. (CAUTION: unless you have a really strong stomach and are resistant to dizziness, the milder version of the "mission space" ride or not riding at all is recommended.) How did you feel as the spaceship took off? _____

_____

4. Since you have considered the tool-making nature of human beings, explore the celebration of some of those inventions. Ride "Test Track" (but pay attention to all of the tests of the automobile you see in the queue) leading up to the ride. What are some of the tests they put automobiles through? _____

_____

_____

5. Ride "Living with the Land" to enjoy the vegetation. For that matter, just take in all of the scenic landscaping of any Disney park. List some plants that are being grown. _____

6. Since you have considered the tool-making nature of human beings, explore the celebration of some of those inventions. Ride "Soarin'." What various types of transportation are you taking? _____

_____

7. Visit "The Seas with Nemo & Friends" attraction. Unfortunately, you will not be able, there, to view what was formerly "The Living Seas" Preshow film. That film has now been replaced with a much less theological Nemo ride. But, consider the sea life. Do you detect any gradual evolution? _____ Explain. _____ Enjoy the underwater creatures of the exhibit.

8. Visit the Mexico Pavilion and look for Kukulkan, the feathery snake god on the columns of the pyramid.

9. Visit the China Pavilion. How is Buddha depicted? What "values" would you think this religion holds? _____

10. Ride the "Maelstrom" at the Norway Pavilion. Be introduced to trolls. Any other gods? _____ . Of what denomination is the church at the pavilion? _____

11. Visit the attraction "The American Adventure" and answer the following:

a. There is mention of the "creator" in what document? _____

b. Make a list of the geniuses you see or hear referenced in the presentation.

_____

_____

_____

_____

c. Why do you think of these individuals as geniuses? What did they "know" that the average human does not? _____

_____

_____

12.   Visit the Italy Pavilion. You will see ancient Roman gods (Neptune) and angels. You will also see saints high atop the columns at the entrance. Can you identify any of them? _____

13.   Visit the Japan Pavilion. What do you think is the cultural religion? _____

14.   Visit the Morocco Pavilion. Can you find any religious symbols? _____

MK:

1.   Since you have considered the tool-making nature of human beings, explore the celebration of some of those inventions, ride "the "Monorail" between EPCOT and MK or from the parking area to the MK. What energy powers the Monorail? _____

2.   Since you have considered the tool-making nature of human beings, explore the celebration of some of those inventions. Ride "The Walt Disney World Railroad." What energy powers the train? _____

      a. What kinds of tools do the natives have? _____

3.   Journey on the "Jungle Cruise." Pay close attention to depictions of the natives. List any tools they are carrying, especially tools for hunting. _____

      a.   There is a large head image at entrance to a temple, Inside is a golden monkey, surrounded by _____, with treasure around him.

4.   Visit "The Hall of Presidents." Clearly, presidents are the top of the hierarchy in the U.S., but do you detect any hierarchy among the various presidents (a top of the top), according to the Disney presentation? Explain. _____

      a. How many presidents are shown there? _____

5.   Visit "The Haunted Mansion." List the explicit "Thou shalt not's" you are confronted with: _____

a.   **Pay close attention to the various depictions of ghosts. Are there such things as ghosts? Defend your position:** _____

_____

b.   **Do you have any religious objections to any part of this ride?**

_____

6.   **Have a snack at (or just a visit to) Pinocchio's Village Haus restaurant. Surrounded by a scene resembling that of Disney's movie, think of the implicit "Thou shalt not's" in the movie, *Pinocchio*:** _____

_____

7.   **Walk through "Cinderella Castle." Note the series of five scenes made of mosaic tiles on the left as you enter from Main Street. The first scene depicts a problem-- Cinderella working among the cinders. What is happening in the three middle scenes?** _____

_____

_____

In the final scene, Cinderella is carried away by her prince on his white horse. Perfection!

8.   **Ride the "Tomorrowland Transit Authority" and pay close attention to the model view of the perfect community, as you approach "Space Mountain." Then, visit Disney's "perfect community"—Celebration, Florida--located directly south of the MK and Disney property, on World Drive. What, in your opinion, makes a community "perfect"?** _____

_____

9.   **Visit the attraction "Carousel of Progress" and answer the following:**

a.   **Make a list of the geniuses you see or hear referenced in the presentation.**

_____

_____

_____

_____

b.   Why do you think of these individuals as geniuses? What did they "know" that the average human does not? _____

_____

_____

_____

10.   Join "Stitch's Great Escape."   Do you detect any evolutionary rhetoric? _____

11.   View the fireworks presentation ("Wishes").   List the nonentities the Disney corporation encourages you to "believe" in—the wishing star, blue fairy, etc.

_____

_____

_____

_____

HS:

1.   Catch a meal (or just visit) at the "Sci-Fi Dine In" restaurant at HS. Study the aliens. Do you notice any signs of an implicit belief in evolution?   What? _____

_____

_____

2.   Since you have considered the tool-making nature of human beings, explore the celebration of some of those inventions. Ride "Star Tours" and join R2-D2 in a (futuristic) space mission. Do the machines humans have made seem human themselves? _____

3.   Ride the "Great Movie Ride" at the studios. Pay attention to the movie trailers from "Alien" and "Fantasia" (specifically, "The Rite of Spring") and see if you see any "powerful" alien creatures in the "Alien" set you ride through. What evidence of evolution do you detect? _____

_____

4.   Visit the attraction "Walt Disney: One Man's Dream" and answer the following:

a. **Make a list of the inventions, innovations, and "creations" of Walt Disney.**

_____

_____

_____

_____

b. **When Walt was a boy, one of his biggest heroes was _____.**
From the 5th grade on up, Walt recalled, "I always came around on his
birthday."

c. **When Walt was growing up, his family was just barely making ends meet.**
On Christmas and birthdays, _____ would always see that
Walt and his sister had a toy.

d. **What, do you think, is the driving motivation for the man who created the**
Disney Empire? _____

_____

e. **What is the glue that holds together everything he built in his lifetime? Why**
did he do all these things? _____

_____

_____

_____

f. **In 1955 Walt had conquered 2 dimensional animation and began to dream**
of a world where humans could actually step into where his characters lived,
perhaps even becoming the characters in the stories. This sounds like
"identification." What rhetorician made identification a major focus of his
work? _____

g.   In the film about his life, Walt uses the (religious) term "blessing" to describe a new development for him—the blessing of size. What was he talking about? _____

5. Visit "Journey into Narnia: Prince Caspian." The C.S. Lewis stories are supposed to hold Christian messages. Do you see any? _____
_____

6. In the "Voyage of the Little Mermaid," Triton, a sea god, finally gives the little mermaid legs. What agency does he use to accomplish this feat? _____
_____

7. Take in the "Indiana Jones Epic Stunt Spectacular." Jones was an archaeologist who studied religious artifacts. Who is the "perfectly evil" force in this attraction?
_____

8. Notice the Sorcerer's Apprentice Hat. It has what heavenly symbols on it? _____ Sorcery is a religion.

9. Ride the "Great Movie Ride." Pay special attention to the Indiana Jones set where Indy is moving the Ark of the Covenant. Notice that on top of the Ark are two golden angels with their wings touching in the middle of the Ark. The place where the wings meet is called the "Mercy Seat." Hebrew theology says that God sits above that seat. Look very carefully above the seat. Do you see anything?_____ Why? _____

a.   Notice the chimney sweeps in the Mary Poppins scene and consider the line of the song "Chim Chim Cheree" that states: "Now as the ladder of life 'as been strung, you may think a sweep's on the bottommost rung." What does that song say about hierarchy? _____
_____

b.   You will see a film clip, at the end, of Moses (Charlton Heston) from the movie *The Ten Commandments*. What is he doing? _____

10. Ride the "Twilight Zone Tower of Terror" and pay close attention to the various depictions of ghosts. What do you think happens to humans after they die? _____

_____

    c. Did you feel that you were going to die when the elevator dropped? _____

11. View "Fantasmic" in the evening. You will experience Mickey Mouse's dream of "Light vs. Darkness." Make a list of Disney's villains portrayed in this presentation.

_____

_____

_____

Do they come close to the concept of perfect evil? How so? _____

_____

AK:

1.   Pay attention to the words cast members use around the Tree of Life. Do any of them say "Viva Gaia"? _____

2.   View the show "It's Tough to Be a Bug" to get a glance at really small animal life. What animal "caught your attention" the most? _____

3.   Take a jeep ride at "Kilimanjaro Safaris" to see a wide variety of creeping things (crocodiles), livestock, and wild animals. Notice the song played on the radio in the Jeep. It is "The Lord's Prayer" in Swahili. What did your guide say to you in Swahili, as you left? _____

    a. List the animals that you encountered. _____

_____

_____

_____

4.   Walk through "Pangani Forest." Is there any evolutionary rhetoric to be found?

_____

5.   Stroll through "Maharajah Jungle Trek." Notice the wild land animals. What animal was most impressive? _____

6.   Visit the show "Flights of Wonder" to become better acquainted with the birds of the air.   What bird flew straight toward the photographers on stage? _____ You will see more birds on your safari and walks through "Pangani Forest" and the "Maharajah Jungle Trek."

7.   See the highest life forms before man—the apes—at "Pangani Forest." Visit the gorillas. Which gorilla do you believe is at the top of the gorilla hierarchy in that collection of gorillas?   Describe the top of the gorilla hierarchy. _____

_____.

8.   Visit the attraction "Dinosaur." There, you will time travel backwards to the Cretaceous Era, which the Disney ride estimates occurred 65 million years ago. According to the ride, the age of the dinosaurs ended because of _____

_____

9.   Hike on the Cretaceous Trail. See the Pachycephalosaurus dinosaur that lived 65 million years ago and become a paleontologist who discovers fascinating fossil dig sites.

10. Enjoy all of the "creatures" in the AK.

Made in the USA
Charleston, SC
20 August 2015